coolcamping
england

Jonathan Knight,
Paul Marsden and Andy Stothert

with additional contributions by Xenia Gregoriadis, Sue Newman and Sam Pow

The publishers assert their right to use
Cool Camping as a trademark of Punk Publishing Ltd.

Cool Camping: England
First edition published in 2006
This second edition published in the United Kingdom in 2008 by
Punk Publishing Ltd
3 The Yard
Pegasus Place
London SE11 5SD

www.punkpublishing.com

www.coolcamping.co.uk

A catalogue record of this book is available from the British Library.
ISBN-13: 978-0-9552036-6-4 2nd edition
(ISBN-13: 978-0-9552036-1-9 1st edition)

10 9 8 7 6 5 4 3 2

Introduction	4	Norfolk	132
Campsite Locator	8	Lincolnshire	144
Cool Camping Top 5	10	Gloucestershire	148
Campsites at a Glance	12	Herefordshire	150
Isles of Scilly	16	Shropshire	158
Cornwall	22	Peak District	166
Devon	46	West Yorkshire	178
Somerset	66	North Yorkshire	180
Wiltshire	74	County Durham	198
Dorset	78	Lancashire	202
New Forest	94	Lake District	204
Isle of Wight	100	Northumberland	236
Sussex	106	Festival Fun	248
Kent	120	Top Tips	254
Essex	128	Credits	256

introduction

Welcome to the second edition of *Cool Camping: England*, updated and revised with 35 brand new campsites for your outdoor pleasure. For those 'originals' who discovered us early, we hope you'll like the update. And if you're new to the whole *Cool Camping* thing, well hello there. Nice of you to join us.

Since the first edition of *Cool Camping: England* came out in 2006 – a quick compilation of favourite sites and personal recommendations – we've realised that many people across Britain share our vision of what constitutes a special campsite. Cracking views is top of the list. Then, in no particular order: woodland sites, remote countryside locations, quiet peaceful hideaways and 'unusual' camping experiences. The latter could be anything from a Romany caravan or an American Airstream trailer to a yurt or tipi. It's great to see so many camping innovations springing up, like the large comfortable, family-style tents available at Feather Down Farm (p144) or the African-style safari experience at Port Lympne Wild Animal Park (p120). Not only are these experiences fun and enjoyable, but they help to introduce the concept of camping and getting outdoors to people who might not have considered it before.

For traditional 'tenters', though, it has become increasingly difficult to find those few special sites. This is partly due to the commercialisation of camping – the transformation of campsites into holiday parks where concrete roads, electric hook-ups and huge static caravans take precedence over the joyous simplicity of untouched countryside. But as the *Cool Camping* revolution gathers pace, farmers and campsite owners are beginning to realise that countryside is king. They don't need to chop down trees to squeeze in more tents – we want to camp in ancient woodlands amongst the mighty oaks and bramble thicket. Nor do they need to invest in clubhouses and restaurants – we'll cook our own food, thanks, and entertain ourselves around the campfire of an evening. Keep it simple, that's what contemporary campers want.

We call it cool camping, but that's just a name we invented for the front cover. Other people call it countryside camping, old-school camping, 'proper' camping... It doesn't really matter what you call it, it's all about escaping the modern world and getting out amongst nature. Most of us have busy, stressful jobs that involve spending our lives cooped up in battery-offices, surrounded by computer screens and RSS feeds. Let's go free range! Let's us breath the air of the countryside! And let's find a nice rural gastropub whilst we're at it.

And so, our mission is to bring you a cherry-picked selection of just the very best campsites in the land, and we've scoured the length and breadth of England to find the campsites and camping experiences worthy of inclusion. Some of the new entries include an incredible sea-view campsite in Dorset with its own private beach (p80), a loveably-chintzy retro trailer-park in Yorkshire (p194) and an eccentrically landscaped coastal site in Cornwall (p28). We've searched the country for gems and we've come up trumps with the crazy wooden wigwams at Pot-a-Doodle Do in Northumberland (p246), the idyllic lakeside rurality at St Ives Farm in Sussex (p112) and, amazingly, a forest campsite just a tube-ride from central London (p128).

We've kept the much-loved and highly useful entries for each site, including 'Nearest Decent Pub' and what to do 'If It Rains' or 'If It's Full'. And there's more practical info on the 35 sites that featured in the original book including new entries for Food and Drink, Public Transport (where convenient) and ideas to Treat Yourself in the local area.

A recent survey suggested that camping was declining in popularity in Britain. On closer inspection, it turned out that the survey focused on caravan parks and the larger, corporately owned operations, where numbers have been falling. But if you talk to farmers and small campsite owners across the country, they'll tell you how the opposite is true for them – how an increase in camping visitors has helped not only their business, but also local food producers, speciality shops and other rural industries. And so the combined economic impact of our simple camping trips is helping to regenerate and reinvigorate forgotten areas of Britain's countryside by investing in the people who care about it most – its long-term residents.

Economics aside, camping is the innocent idyll, the ultimate outdoorsy summer holiday and the perfect tonic to big-city life. And *Cool Camping: England* is where you'll find those truly special escapes. So, take your pick of the pitches and head for the hills. Enjoy!

campsite locator

MAP REF	CAMPSITE	LOCATION	PAGE
1	Troytown Farm	Isles of Scilly	16
2	Bryher	Isles of Scilly	20
3	Treen Farm	Cornwall	22
4	Ayr Holiday Park	Cornwall	26
5	Henry's	Cornwall	28
6	Dennis Cove	Cornwall	32
7	Porth Joke	Cornwall	36
8	South Penquite	Cornwall	40
9	Bay View Farm	Cornwall	42
10	Slapton Sands	Devon	46
11	Cockingford Farm	Devon	50
12	Croyde Bay	Devon	52
13	Lundy Island	Devon	56
14	Little Meadow	Devon	58
15	Cloud Farm	Devon	62
16	Greenacres	Somerset	66
17	Batcombe Vale	Somerset	70
18	Stowford Manor Farm	Wiltshire	74
19	Sea Barn Farm	Dorset	78
20	Eweleaze Farm	Dorset	80
21	Downshay Farm	Dorset	84
22	Tom's Field	Dorset	88
23	Burnbake	Dorset	90
24	Tom's Field	New Forest	94
25	Roundhill	New Forest	96
26	Grange Farm	Isle of Wight	100
27	Vintage Vacations	Isle of Wight	102
28	Blackberry Wood	Sussex	106
29	Heaven Farm	Sussex	110
30	St Ives Farm	Sussex	112
31	Sussex Tipis	Sussex	116
32	Livingstone Lodge	Kent	120
33	The Warren	Kent	124
34	Debden House	Essex	128
35	Clippesby Hall	Norfolk	132
36	Deer's Glade	Norfolk	136
37	Pinewoods	Norfolk	138
38	Deepdale Farm	Norfolk	140
39	Feather Down Farm	Lincolnshire	144
40	Bracelands	Gloucestershire	148
41	Woodland Tipis	Herefordshire	150
42	Eastnor Castle	Herefordshire	154
43	Middle Woodbatch Farm	Shropshire	158
44	Small Batch	Shropshire	162
45	Longnor Wood	Peak District	166
46	North Lees	Peak District	170
47	Fieldhead	Peak District	174
48	Upper Booth Farm	Peak District	176
49	Jerusalem Farm	West Yorkshire	178
50	Gordale Scar	North Yorkshire	180
51	Knight Stainforth	North Yorkshire	184
52	Spiers House	North Yorkshire	188
53	Hooks House Farm	North Yorkshire	190
54	La Rosa	North Yorkshire	194
55	Highside Farm	County Durham	198
56	Gibraltar Farm	Lancashire	202
57	Full Circle	Lake District	204
58	Low Wray	Lake District	208
59	Baysbrown Farm	Lake District	210
60	Turner Hall Farm	Lake District	214
61	Wasdale Head	Lake District	218
62	Syke Farm	Lake District	220
63	Stonethwaite	Lake District	222
64	Gillside Farm	Lake District	224
65	Side Farm	Lake District	228
66	The Quiet Site	Lake District	232
67	Hadrian's Wall	Northumberland	236
68	Demesne Farm	Northumberland	238
69	Beadnell Bay	Northumberland	242
70	Pot-a-Doodle Do	Northumberland	246

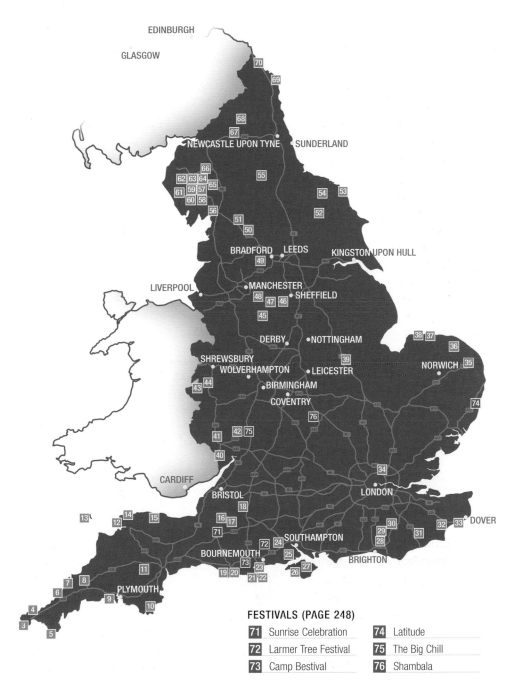

EDINBURGH

GLASGOW

70

69

68
67
NEWCASTLE UPON TYNE   SUNDERLAND

66
62 63 64 65   55
61 59 57   54   53
60 58
56   52
51
50
BRADFORD LEEDS
49   KINGSTON UPON HULL
LIVERPOOL
MANCHESTER
48 47 46 • SHEFFIELD
45

DERBY • NOTTINGHAM   38 37
36
SHREWSBURY   39   35
WOLVERHAMPTON • LEICESTER   NORWICH
44
43   • BIRMINGHAM
• COVENTRY   74
76
41 42 75
40

CARDIFF
BRISTOL   LONDON
18   34
13   14   DOVER
12   15   30   32 33
16 17   29   31
71   28
72   24
BOURNEMOUTH   SOUTHAMPTON
73   25   BRIGHTON
11   19 20 23   27
7   21 22   26
8
PLYMOUTH
9
10
4
2   3
1   5

FESTIVALS (PAGE 248)
71 Sunrise Celebration   74 Latitude
72 Larmer Tree Festival   75 The Big Chill
73 Camp Bestival   76 Shambala

1 2
3 4

cool camping top 5

And now, ladies and gentlemen, the moment you've all been waiting for (cue fanfare)... the Oscars of the camping world, the Turner prize for tenters, the 'Brits' and the 'Mobos' rolled into one... no, not the 'Bobos' – it's the Cool Camping Top 5.

1 Henry's, Cornwall   p28

A weird and wonderful campsite, eccentrically landscaped with both Cornish and tropical influences – and within a splash of Cornwall's spectacular coast.

2 Downshay Farm, Dorset   p84

We're suckers for views, and Downshay Farm delivers with a castle-tastic Dorset vista. Lovin' your work, guys.

3 Batcombe Vale, Somerset   p70

A slice of pure Shangri La in the midst of rural Somerset. Be prepared for some serious relaxation, extra special views and even a bit o' boating.

4 Side Farm, Lake District   p228

This place was at the front of the queue when the Lake District views were handed out. We've got one word for you: wow!

5= La Rosa, North Yorkshire   p194

Camping kitsch in quirky caravans complete with far-out interiors. If all caravans looked like this, the world would be a better place.

5= Blackberry Wood, Sussex   p106

Straight in at number 1 in the last edition. Still a lovely site, recently improved with new loos.

campsites at a glance

STUNNING VIEWS PAGE

1	Troytown Farm	16
2	Bryher	20
4	Ayr Holiday Park	26
5	Henry's	28
6	Dennis Cove	32
9	Bay View Farm	42
10	Slapton Sands	46
14	Little Meadow	58
19	Sea Barn Farm	78
20	Eweleaze Farm	80
21	Downshay Farm	84
26	Grange Farm	100
32	Livingstone Lodge	120
33	The Warren	124
43	Middle Woodbatch Farm	158
50	Gordale Scar	180
53	Hooks House Farm	190
58	Low Wray	208
59	Baysbrown Farm	210
61	Wasdale Head	218
62	Syke Farm	220
63	Stonethwaite	222
64	Gillside Farm	224
65	Side Farm	228

FOR FIRST-TIME CAMPERS

4	Ayr Holiday Park	26
5	Henry's	28
10	Slapton Sands	46
19	Sea Barn Farm	78
27	Vintage Vacations	102
31	Sussex Tipis	116
35	Clippesby Hall	132

36	Deer's Glade	136
37	Pinewoods	138
38	Deepdale Farm	140
39	Feather Down Farm	144
40	Bracelands	148
41	Woodland Tipis	150
45	Longnor Wood	166
51	Knight Stainforth	184
66	The Quiet Site	232

MIDDLE OF NOWHERE

1	Troytown Farm	16
2	Bryher	20
8	South Penquite	40
11	Cockingford Farm	50
13	Lundy Island	56
17	Batcombe Vale	70
30	St Ives Farm	112
50	Gordale Scar	180
52	Spiers House	188
55	Highside Farm	198
60	Turner Hall Farm	214
61	Wasdale Head	218
62	Syke Farm	220
63	Stonethwaite	222
67	Hadrian's Wall	236

BEACH WITHIN REACH

1	Troytown Farm	16
2	Bryher	20
3	Treen Farm	22
4	Ayr Holiday Park	26
5	Henry's	28
6	Dennis Cove	32

7	Porth Joke	36
9	Bay View Farm	42
10	Slapton Sands	46
12	Croyde Bay	52
20	Eweleaze Farm	80
23	Burnbake	90
26	Grange Farm	100
33	The Warren	124
37	Pinewoods	138
53	Hooks House Farm	190
56	Gibraltar Farm	202
69	Beadnell Bay	242
70	Pot-a-Doodle Do	246

SURF'S UP

3	Treen Farm	22
4	Ayr Holiday Park	26
12	Croyde Bay	52
26	Grange Farm	100
27	Vintage Vacations	102

SOMETHING DIFFERENT

5	Henry's	28
8	South Penquite	40
17	Batcombe Vale	70
18	Stowford Manor Farm	74
27	Vintage Vacations	102
31	Sussex Tipis	116
32	Livingstone Lodge	120
39	Feather Down Farm	144
41	Woodland Tipis	150
54	La Rosa	194
57	Full Circle	204
70	Pot-a-Doodle Do	246

COOL FOR CAMPFIRES — PAGE

5	Henry's	28
7	Porth Joke	36
11	Cockingford Farm	50
20	Eweleaze Farm	80
30	St Ives Farm	112
31	Sussex Tipis	116
34	Debden House	128
41	Woodland Tipis	150
43	Middle Woodbatch Farm	158

FOREST FUN

24	Tom's Field	94
25	Roundhill	96
28	Blackberry Wood	106
36	Deer's Glade	136
40	Bracelands	148
41	Woodland Tipis	150
46	North Lees	170
52	Spiers House	188

LAKESIDE CHILLING

17	Batcombe Vale	70
30	St Ives Farm	112
36	Deer's Glade	136
37	Pinewoods	138
58	Low Wray	208
65	Side Farm	228

FOR CAR-LESS CAMPERS

4	Ayr Holiday Park	26
5	Henry's	28
6	Dennis Cove	32

32	Livingstone Lodge	120
36	Deer's Glade	136
42	Eastnor Castle	154
44	Small Batch	162
47	Fieldhead	174
48	Upper Booth Farm	176
56	Gibraltar Farm	202

WALK THIS WAY

5	Henry's	28
7	Porth Joke	36
10	Slapton Sands	46
11	Cockingford Farm	50
14	Little Meadow	58
15	Cloud Farm	62
16	Greenacres	66
17	Batcombe Vale	70
20	Eweleaze Farm	80
22	Tom's Field	88
23	Burnbake	90
30	St Ives Farm	112
40	Bracelands	148
42	Eastnor Castle	154
43	Middle Woodbatch Farm	158
44	Small Batch	162
45	Longnor Wood	166
46	North Lees	170
47	Fieldhead	174
48	Upper Booth Farm	176
49	Jerusalem Farm	178
50	Gordale Scar	180
53	Hooks House Farm	190
57	Full Circle	204

58	Low Wray	208
59	Baysbrown Farm	210
60	Turner Hall Farm	214
61	Wasdale Head	218
62	Syke Farm	220
64	Gillside Farm	224
65	Side Farm	228
66	The Quiet Site	232
67	Hadrian's Wall	236
68	Demesne Farm	238
69	Beadnell Bay	242

GOOD FOR KIDS

5	Henry's	28
10	Slapton Sands	46
11	Cockingford Farm	50
16	Greenacres	66
20	Eweleaze Farm	80
23	Burnbake	90
29	Heaven Farm	110
32	Livingstone Lodge	120
41	Woodland Tipis	150
43	Middle Woodbatch Farm	158
44	Small Batch	162

MIDGE WARNING!

47	Fieldhead	174
49	Jerusalem Farm	178
52	Spiers House	188
55	Highside Farm	198
58	Low Wray	208
66	The Quiet Site	232

troytown farm

If camping on the tiny island of St Agnes isn't exciting enough, it's certainly an adventure getting there. Take your pick from a boat, plane or helicopter ride for the journey to the Isles of Scilly's main islands, Tresco or St Mary's. The plane has the edge for maximum thrill, a tiny eight-seater bouncing about on the winds. Bag one of the front seats, inches from the whirring propellers, for a bird's-eye view of the 100-odd islands that make up this archipelago.

Then it's on to a catamaran for the trip to St Agnes. If it's a bright day, you'll be greeted by the almost Mediterranean sight of boats moored on the turquoise waters of Porth Conger as you arrive. Next is a tractor ride – for your luggage at least. Most people choose to let their bags go ahead and walk the 20 minutes to the campsite, a scenic stroll that provides a stunning introduction to the island.

At just one mile in diameter, St Agnes is one of the smallest inhabited islands of the Scilly archipelago. It's a beautiful, rugged place that has seen little change since Celtic times, a forgotten outpost of England's west. The majority of the island's 70 inhabitants work in flower farming during the winter months as they have done for generations, although tourism is now as important to the economy. Even so, there are only a handful of B&Bs on the island – most people come to stay at Troytown Farm, England's westernmost campsite.

Its position couldn't be any more remote or spectacular. The campsite clings to the western foreshore of the island, just feet away from the rock-calmed Atlantic waters that look as if they might engulf the campsite at high tide. To one side, a beautiful curve of sand at Periglis Beach extends into the sea. To the other, bold, intriguing rock formations add interest to the heather-covered coastal landscape. It's a magical wilderness that feels like the ends of the earth. In fact, it is almost at the ends of the earth; the nearest neighbours to the southwest are New Yorkers.

There are small, separate fieldlets with low hedges and walls offering a certain amount of protection from the elements, but this can be a windy island so come prepared. When the sun shines, though, this place is perfect. You can play in the rock pools, spot the rare, migrating birds or just sling up a hammock and listen to the waves gently lapping on the foreshore. At night, the lack of light pollution affords incredible views of the Milky Way and dazzling displays of shooting stars. Isolation is this island's greatest asset, so bring a love of nature and plenty of books to read.

The island may be remote, but it's fairly self-sufficient. Troytown Farm has a small dairy herd producing milk and cream for the island. They also rear pigs and grow vegetables to provide campers with food, so most survival essentials are available at the farmhouse and on-site shop.

The other of life's necessities is available by the pint at The Turks Head in Porth Conger, the island's only pub. Perched on the hillside overlooking the bay and the adjacent islet of The Gugh, it might just win the prize for best beer garden view in England.

St Agnes is also blessed with some fantastic beaches. As well as Periglis Beach near the campsite, there's the small, sheltered beach at Cove Vean on the eastern shore and a sandbar at Porth Conger, where you can splash about in the waves or walk across to The Gugh at low tide. But for great sunset views, head back to Periglis – and see if you can't spot the Statue of Liberty in the distance.

THE UPSIDE: Extreme Atlantic isolation, one of England's most naturally beautiful campsites.
THE DOWNSIDE: Not easy to get to!
THE DAMAGE: From £6.50 to £8 per person per night. Luggage transportation £2.50 per person.
THE FACILITIES: Traditional-style granite building houses good facilities, including toilets, showers (tokens required), coin-operated washing machines and dryers, shaver points and baby-changing facilities. There's an on-site shop.

NEAREST DECENT PUB: The Turks Head, Porth Conger has great food and beer, surpassed only by the view.
FOOD AND DRINK: The farm shop on-site sells its own dairy products, veg and some meat.
IF IT RAINS: If the weather gets really bad (and it has been known to be windy here!) Troytown Farm also offer self-catering accommodation in a chalet and cottage.
TREAT YOURSELF: To a trip to see local seals and puffins with Island Wildlife Tours (01742 422212).

GETTING THERE: Contact Isles of Scilly Travel (0845 710 5555; www.ios-travel.co.uk) for plane and boat travel or British International (01736 363871; www.islesofscillyhelicopter.com) for helicopter services. Contact Troytown Farm for details of transportation to the campsite.
OPEN: Mar–Oct; winter by arrangement. Advance bookings essential during Jul & Aug.
IF IT'S FULL: The *Cool Camping* site at Bryher (p20) is just a boat trip away.

| **Troytown Campsite**, Troytown Farm, St Agnes, Isles of Scilly TR22 0PL | t | 01720 422360 | w | www.troytown.co.uk |

bryher

The tiny island of Bryher, Isles of Scilly, has two distinct faces. To the south and east, calm blue waters fill the narrow, sheltered channel between the island and its larger cousin, Tresco. Boats come and go whilst sunbathers enjoy the sandy beaches at Green Bay and the secluded cove of Rushy Bay. The northwestern shores, however, are a jagged jumble of weather-torn rocks, beaten and broken by the relentless Atlantic waves. Gales sometimes lash this coast with thousand-ton breakers, and places like Badplace Hill and Hell Bay have earned their names through reputation.

Such schizophrenic characteristics make this island special. The sandy-beach bays to the island's south are backed by dunes and provide ample opportunity for sunbathing, swimming and snorkelling, although the water can be a little nippy. Just beyond sits Samson Hill, the southernmost point of the island, with far-reaching views across the Scillies. The exposed, heather-covered plateau at the northern end of the island is dotted with prehistoric burial cairns.

Situated a short climb uphill from the boat jetty, Bryher campsite has elevated views of the harbour, Hangman Island and Tresco, yet occupies a sheltered spot between two higher hills. It's tents only at this discreet site that blends effortlessly into the landscape of the island.

It's undoubtedly a beautiful spot. But to really see the best side of this isle of contrasts, visit in the spring or summer when warm, sunny days turn Bryher into an idyllic island paradise.

THE UPSIDE: Remote island camping with spectacular views.
THE DOWNSIDE: It's a bit far for the weekend.
THE DAMAGE: £8.50 per person per night.
THE FACILITIES: Excellent toilets, basins and free showers. Coin-operated hairdryer and shaver point along with washing machine and dryer. Freezer for ice packs. Tractor service for luggage from the quay (bookable in advance).
NEAREST DECENT PUB: The cosy Fraggle Rock (01720 422222), Scilly's smallest pub, is just a few minutes' walk down the hill towards the quay. The contemporary Hell Bay Hotel (01720 422947; www.hellbay.co.uk) has an outside bar deck overlooking the sea and outstanding local seafood in the restaurant. Dinner reservations essential.
FOOD AND DRINK: Catch a boat to Highertown on St Martins to sample some of the wares at St Martin's bakery (01720 423444).
IF IT RAINS: See local artists' work at the Golden Eagle Studio (01720 422671) near the Hell Bay Hotel. Otherwise, jump on a boat to visit the larger towns on St Mary's and Tresco.
TREAT YOURSELF: To sea views of the island from your very own catamaran; contact Bennett Boatyard (07979 393206).
GETTING THERE: Contact Isles of Scilly Travel (0845 710 5555; www.ios-travel.co.uk) for plane and boat travel or British International (01736 363871; www.islesofscillyhelicopter.com) for helicopter services.
OPEN: Mar–Oct.
IF IT'S FULL: There's the equally beautiful Cool Camping campsite on nearby St Agnes (p16).

Bryher Campsite, Bryher, Isles of Scilly TR23 0PR | t | 01720 422886 | w | www.bryhercampsite.co.uk

treen farm

Beach babes and sun lovers, oil up and grab your flip-flops – Treen Farm campsite, three miles shy of Land's End, is just a towel's throw from some of England's finest beaches.

Treen Farm has been in the Halls family for time eternal. During the last war, one of the fields on the cliff top was commandeered by the army as a communications post. A few military buildings were constructed on the land, rendering it useless for farming – but perfect for camping.

Since then, campers and cows have co-existed at Treen Farm and the camping field has been updated. A fancy tap with running water was installed in 1974, and there are now even toilets and hot showers. The spacious site is a comfortable field's length back from the cliff top so isn't overly exposed, but there are sea glimpses over the hedges that gives the site a sense of place.

What you can't see are the beaches, but you don't have to go far. The nearest is Pedn Vounder, a tiny, isolated cove of golden sand accessed by a 10-minute cliff-top walk and a five-minute rocky scramble from the campsite. The difficult position means it's

never busy, but it does get cut off at high tide, so keep an eye out. At low tide, you can walk along the sand to Green Bay and the larger Porthcurno beach at the western edge of the bay, a popular family favourite and much more accessible. There's a car park at Porthcurno for day trippers, as well as shops, restaurants and a pub. On a hot summer's day it can be extremely crowded, but the crowds tend not to venture round the bay to the quieter beaches. This stretch of coast is characterised by a series of sharp, triangular coves cut into the grey, granite cliffs, the jagged, weather-lined rocks contrasting with the soft sand beneath. The beaches are sheltered and swim-friendly, with lifeguards on duty at Porthcurno during the summer months.

If that's not enough beach for your buck, it's just 10 minutes in the car to Sennen on the north coast, where Whitesands Bay provides a huge, sweeping arch of yellow, fluffy sand and one of Cornwall's best surfing spots. Bliss. Bucket-and-spade summer days don't come any better than this.

Treen used to be a popular tourist destination thanks to Logan Rock, a 70-tonne lump of granite naturally balanced so that it could be rocked back and forth. People came from far and wide to try their strength at rocking (or as they used to say, log'n) the stone, until in 1824 testosterone and bravado got the better of a bunch of drunken sailors who pushed it clean over into the sea. Local residents were outraged at this act of mindless vandalism and the ringleader of the sorry gang was ordered by the Admiralty to return the stone to its rightful position at his own expense. It was a project that took considerably more time and energy than the original drunken prank, and nearly bankrupted the young sailor. Needless to say, the rocking action has never been the same since.

Thankfully, modern-day attractions in the area are enough to topple a wobbling rock from its position as principal tourist draw. Aside from the beaches and coastline, diversions include the worthwhile Porthcurno Telegraph Museum, telling the story of the first international telegraph system that began its underwater journey here, and the Minack Theatre, an open-air auditorium cut into the cliffs west of Porthcurno. Its dramatic cliff-side setting and the backdrop of the crashing sea makes the Minack a unique theatre experience – and like the fine beaches here, it shouldn't be missed.

THE UPSIDE: Walking distance to outstanding Cornish beaches.

THE DOWNSIDE: No pre-booking.

THE DAMAGE: From £11.50 per night for 2 adults with a small tent and car. Adults are £4, under-4s free, children (4–10) £1.50 and 11–16s £2. Tents and motorhomes only.

THE FACILITIES: Showers (token operated, 25p for 5 minutes), toilets (including disabled facilities), laundry and washing-up area. The shop sells most things you might need. A pizza van sometimes appears on a Friday night.

NEAREST DECENT PUB: The Logan Rock Inn (01736 810495) in Treen is a friendly pub selling St Austell Ales and a wide range of meals, with plenty of local fish and seafood options.

FOOD AND DRINK: Sample some of the delicious unpasteurised Treen Farm milk, straight from the cows. They sell yoghurt and organic eggs, too.

IF IT RAINS: Indoor attractions abound at Penzance (12 miles) and Land's End (3 miles).

TREAT YOURSELF: To a meal (or a night if you're feeling flash) at 17th-century The Abbey (01736 351163) in Penzance, which has a Michelin

starred restaurant as well as rooms and suites.

GETTING THERE: Take the A30 southwest from Penzance, then turn onto the B3283 through St Buryan to Treen. The campsite reception is at the shop in the village.

PUBLIC TRANSPORT: From Penzance train station catch the bus to Land's End. Get off at the foot of the hill in Treen, and it's a 5-minute walk.

OPEN: Apr–Oct. No pre-booking.

IF IT'S FULL: Trevedra Farm Campsite (01736 871818) 10 minutes drive away at Sennen has great beach access and is popular with surfers.

Treen Farm Campsite, Treen, St Levan, Penzance, Cornwall TR19 6LF

| t | 01736 810273 | w | www.treenfarmcampsite.co.uk |

ayr holiday park

Artists have been gravitating towards the seaside town of St Ives since the Second World War when sculptor Barbara Hepworth, abstract painter Ben Nicholson and Russian sculptor Naum Gabo all made it their home, attracted by the quality of light, a bustling scene and stimulating coast and countryside.

In 1993, Tate St Ives opened a substantial and impressive gallery, recognising the contribution of the St Ives School to the British art scene. The building itself overlooks sandy Porthmeor Beach, the main town beach with good surfschools and spectacular sunsets. This bay is also the location of our favourite campsite of the many around St Ives – Ayr Holiday Park.

Everything about this campsite is organised and professional, from the soft-landing children's play area to the outside showers for wetsuits. They've really thought about the guests, but unfortunately all this luxury comes at a price. But when you consider its location, the cost is partially justifiable.

Make the most of the site's proximity to the town and stroll down the hill to find wide open beaches, trendy bars and cafés, any number of restaurants from chip-cheap fish shops to contemporary fusion affairs and, of course, the galleries. St Ives is a delightful blend of working fishing port, holiday resort and traditional Cornish town. And, for a town steeped in creativity, they've certainly got the art of camping just right.

THE UPSIDE: The views; a 5-minute walk to town.
THE DOWNSIDE: Expensive, and they pack in the punters for peak season.
THE DAMAGE: Ouch! Two adults with a tent and car are £27 per night and children are £3 each. Two backpackers in a tent pay £16.50.
THE FACILITIES: Magnificent showers, plenty of hot water, a kids' playground, laundrette, games room, wi-fi and direct access to the coastal path.
NEAREST DECENT PUB: St Ives is full of lovely old pubs including The Sloop Inn (01736 796584), a 14th-century inn right on the harbour.

FOOD AND DRINK: The Cornish Deli (01736 795100) in St Ives stocks produce from Cornwall and the West Country. Visit Bill and Flo's farm shop (01736 798885) in Lelant for their own veg, local meat, cheese, honey, cider and apple juice.
IF IT RAINS: Don your waterproofs and walk to Tate St Ives (01736 796226).
TREAT YOURSELF: To a day trip by helicopter to the Isles of Scilly from Penzance (01736 363871).
GETTING THERE: Central St Ives is closed to traffic. Following signs for St Ives from the A30, take the B3311 then B3306 to town, then follow

the brown campsite signs to Ayr and Porthmeor Beach. The entrance lies at a sharp S-bend.
PUBLIC TRANSPORT: Catch the train to St Ives and then a taxi to the site. Or you could catch a bus from Redruth, Penzance, Camborne or Truro; the bus station is just next to the station car park.
OPEN: All year.
IF IT'S FULL: Although not in town, Gwithian Farm Campsite (01736 753127) is popular for its proximity to a huge surfing beach. It's about 20 minutes' drive from St Ives.

Ayr Holiday Park, St Ives, Cornwall TR26 1EJ | t | 01736 795855 | w | www.ayrholidaypark.co.uk

henry's

Henry's is different. There is no other way to describe it. The campsite, situated at Caerthillian Farm in the very centre of Lizard village, is the most southerly campsite in mainland Britain. And it's been here for donkey's years. It was certainly here before the Second World War, and probably even before that. Back then it was just a normal campsite and it remained so until the present family guardians, Ron and Jo Lyne, took over from Ron's dad Henry nearly 20 years ago. We asked Ron exactly what he is trying to achieve at Henry's and he muttered something like 'I want it to be like a garden'. It does have the feel of a garden, but there is so much more going on here.

The impression the place gives is that Ron is, at heart, an artist, or perhaps more accurately a landscape artist. An inquisitive stroll through the site, peering into all the nooks and crannies, reveals a complex arrangement of ethereal-looking standing stones and a series of monumental Cornish walls – granite sides with a living core. The sub-tropical plants are an astounding mixture right through the site, but again, they aren't really arranged in garden mode – more in a way to bring out their natural relationship with the Cornish granite. Enough of this theorising about what Ron intended with his years of back-breaking labours, for as you'll see the results are astounding.

Campers who come to Henry's generally return time and time again, but not everybody gets on with the unisex ablutional arrangements, nor the outdoor washing-up sink, which is being invaded by alien-looking plants. Nor indeed by the eccentric former shipping-container loo block, which is painted a very bright blue inside. One of the outside loos is a startling orange hue and, odd that it sounds, is the most popular seat in the house. It's all a bit rambling, and all very well maintained – but different. And speaking of different there's hens, pigs and ponies around and about. The site is open all year, and during the height of the season Ron and Jo also run a small shop in the barn, supplying everything from a car fuse, through to hot cups of tea and eggs from the hens wandering around the site.

Henry's ambience springs from the art and natural sculpture that has been thoughtfully positioned in every corner of the site. New projects include an amphitheatre (made of railway sleepers with a huge central fire-pit), a tennis court and the works of a local sculptor on the site.

The surrounding coastal landscape is even more amazing than the job Ron has done on the site itself, and it has been the inspiration for the way Henry's has evolved over the years. The most notable chunk of coastal scenery hereabouts is Kynance Cove; this iconic place is a 20-minute walk from

the site. Nearer, but not nearly so beautiful, is Lizard Point – with Britain's most southerly café and Gifte Shoppe, whilst in the opposite direction, away from the Atlantic gales, the thatched cottages run down to Church Cove.

It's true that there are any number of campsites in this area, handy for Cornwall's dramatic coastal scenery, but Henry's is the only one with added quirk and eccentricity. A special place indeed.

THE UPSIDE: Quirky, eccentric, beautiful landscaping, the animals, the glorious Lizard peninsula and the folk running the site.

THE DOWNSIDE: The unisex toilet blocks aren't everyone's cup of tea.

THE DAMAGE: Adults £6–7 per night and children £2–3 per night, depending on season.

THE FACILITIES: Scattered, painted in eye-piercingly bright hues, open-air washing-up, unisex arrangements but include toilets, showers, shop, campers' lounge, fire grates and electric hook-ups.

NEAREST DECENT PUB: Less than a 10-minute walk is the trendy Witchball Bar and Restaurant (01326 290662), which offers a wide selection of

good food. And in the village centre is the Regent Café (01326 290483) – nothing short of a national institution and gourmet experience.

FOOD AND DRINK: Head for one (or more) of Anne's Pasties in Lizard village. If you fancy fish on the BBQ, then go meet the fishermen at Cadgwith Cove, who have a cooperative shop where the fish can be bought as soon as they're off the boats. And if ice cream's your thing, then make your way to celebrated organic Roskilly's Ice Cream at Roskilly's Farm near Coverack (01326 280479).

IF IT RAINS: For a totally unique experience, head to Cornish Camels (01326 231119) where there are, you guessed it, camels; but there's also a

café, organic food and craft shop. And go see the cute seals at the National Seal Sanctuary (01326 221874) in the picturesque Helston estuary.

TREAT YOURSELF: To some local crab and lobster at 'Bernies' shop in the street next to the site.

GETTING THERE: Take the A30 all the way through Cornwall to Penzance. Then, go on the A394 to Helston, and then the A3083 to Lizard. The campsite is accessed from the far side of the car park at the Lizard.

OPEN: All year.

IF IT'S FULL: Teneriffe Farm (01326 240293) near Mullion isn't as interesting but it's cheap and in a great location near the coast.

Henry's Campsite, Caerthillian Farm, The Lizard, Helston, Cornwall TR12 7NX

| | t | 01326 290596 | w | www.henryscampsite.co.uk |

dennis cove

Cornwall has been savaged by waves. In the 1970s and early 1980s, waves of tourists descended on the Cornish coast for their annual fortnight of fun, emptying their pockets at flashing-light amusement halls and filling themselves dizzy with ice creams and pasties. Then during the 1980s the waves of tourists receded, as people looked further afield to the exotic charms of Spain and beyond. In an age of package discounts and cheap flights, Cornwall just didn't cut it. It was out of favour and out of fashion.

Now, Cornwall is once again a sought-after destination and right at the forefront of this Cornish revival was Padstow, a fishing port on the dramatic north coast. The Padstow success story was helped by its most famous resident, celebrity chef Rick Stein. It all started with The Seafood Restaurant, his award-winning Padstow eatery that quickly gained a reputation for intricate and innovative dishes. Then came his deli, a bistro, a café, a hotel, a posh fish & chip shop down by the quayside and the popular Padstow Seafood School. Stein's mini-empire raised the profile of Padstow, transforming it into Cornwall's gastronomic capital. Jamie Oliver jumped on the bandwagon, too, with his Fifteen restaurant at Watergate Bay, just down the coast.

It has also altered perceptions of the wider area from a slow backwater to the home of some of the world's best seafood, fresh off the boat. And it's a success story that has encouraged others in the regional tourist industry to look beyond arcades and pasty shops to attract today's sophisticated and demanding holidaymakers.

Even without the flashy food, Padstow is a charming place. At its heart is the busy harbour, buzzing with activity year-round as the fishermen bring in the catch. If you fancy your chances, you can book a boat from the harbour and go mackerel fishing for dinner. A short walk over the headland from the port, you'll find an amazing expanse of sandy beach which opens up at low tide to provide plenty of room for everyone, even on the busiest summer days. This isn't coastal beach but The Camel Estuary – you can see across to the town of Rock on the other side.

Padstow is also the western starting point of the Camel Trail, an easy walking and cycling route that follows the Camel Estuary inland to Wadebridge, then continues alongside the River Camel to Poley's Bridge. For most of its 17 miles it's incredibly scenic (The Camel Estuary is an

Area of Outstanding Natural Beauty) and completely car-free, making it a very popular route in summer when hundreds of bikes and cyclists descend on Padstow. The route forms part of The Cornish Way, a huge 200-mile cycle network that criss-crosses the county from Bude to Land's End.

At the start of The Camel Trail, just south of the fishing port, is Dennis Cove campsite. It's a small, well-cared-for family site close to the town and handy for all the attractions. The philosophy here is 'simple camping'; there are just five electric hook-ups provided for visitors and a well-maintained shower block. Aside from that, the campsite is essentially two fields of

green grass, albeit in a great location and with some commanding views across the Camel Estuary.

The lower field is open all season with trees and hedges providing shelter. It can get a bit squashed down here in the busy months, so a better bet is to make for the upper overflow field, a vast expanse of grass without designated pitch markings. It's further from the amenities and more exposed, being on the higher ground, but the views across the estuary are simply knock-out.

With a BBQ, a bag of fresh Padstow fish and a view like this, who needs posh restaurants?

THE UPSIDE: Glorious views and well-located for The Camel Trail, Cornish Coastal Footpath, beaches and the town.

THE DOWNSIDE: Lower field can be cramped in peak times, with pitches very close together.

THE DAMAGE: A tent, car and 2 people will set you back £12.70–16.70, depending on the season. Families and couples only, no groups.

THE FACILITIES: Simple amenities block (showers cost extra), dishwashing and laundry facilities. Bicycle hire is available in town.

NEAREST DECENT PUB: The London Inn (01841 532554) on Lanadwell Street does traditional pub grub; The Shipwrights (01841 532451) down by the old harbour is a good place to watch the world go by on a summer's day.

FOOD AND DRINK: Padstow Farm Shop (01841 533060) at Trethillick Farm on the outskirts of Padstow have stacks of locally produced food and also supply local 'celebrity' restaurants.

IF IT RAINS: The waterproof biomes at the Eden Project (01726 811911) are only a 25-minute drive away.

TREAT YOURSELF: To a table at The Seafood Restaurant (01841 532700).

GETTING THERE: Entering Padstow on the A389, turn right at Tesco, drive down the hill then turn right on to Dennis Lane and continue to the end.

PUBLIC TRANSPORT: From Bodmin Parkway train station, get the bus to Padstow and then walk.

OPEN: Easter–Sep. Book well in advance.

IF IT'S FULL: Next door is the tent-only Dennis Farm campsite (01841 533513), another great site right on the edge of the estuary.

Dennis Cove Camping, Dennis Lane, Padstow, Cornwall PL28 8DR | t | 01841 532349 | w | www.denniscove.co.uk

porth joke

The *raison d'être* of *Cool Camping* is to celebrate the nation's wide diversity of campsites. But it goes much further and deeper because we want to bring an increased awareness to a small number of sites that offer something remarkable or unique and to campers who want an experience rather than just somewhere to pitch the tent.

Some campsites have been a bit busier since appearing in *Cool Camping*, and that simple fact meant that Bob and Angela Harty, who own this unique site, were slightly reluctant to include Porth Joke in any publication that may potentially damage the seclusion and atmosphere of this hidden paradise. The truth is that it is already as busy as they want it to be, and securing a pitch here in mid-summer is less likely than a very big win on the lottery. But during the peripheral months of May, June or September – well, you never know.

So, what can you expect to find if your number comes up in the camping lottery and there is a vacancy? The honest answer is everything and nothing. If you're looking for easy access, shiny brand-new facilities and plenty of nearby entertainment or eating-out opportunities, then Porth Joke

will disappoint. But, if a small, secluded slice of seaside heaven is what you seek then this out of the way place cannot fail to delight you.

The location, just four miles from Newquay (Cornwall's capital of tack and tourism) is surprising. Even more surprising is that the site is along a narrow, bumpy, sandy track through the dunes and almost a mile from the nearest public road. There are no signs directing the blessed few to Porth Joke, and no indication, until you stumble onto it, that anything exists down this scenic road to nowhere. But there it is, a tiny campsite, sheltered by the dunes from the wrath of the Atlantic, which is just a few hundred metres away.

For a young family who want a simple seaside holiday in totally unspoilt surroundings and with nothing more than the sea, sand and surf to fill their days, then Porth Joke cannot be bettered. The singular attempt at children's entertainment is the huge sandpit in the centre of the site, and plans are to replenish this with a 'bring a bucket from the beach' campaign. Such simple pleasures are what makes this place the stuff of seaside camping dreams. Outside the school holiday period, of course.

It's a lot easier to venture out of Porth Joke on foot, than driving back along that bumpy track, and it's a bracing but beautiful cliff walk of about two miles to the totally sublime Holywell Bay, and another mile or so to the village. Continuing the seaside march on through Holywell will soon bring the endless sands and roaring surf of Perranporth within view. In the other direction from the site lies the equally stunning Crantock beach and then, across the river, the bright lights of Surf City itself, Newquay. It's only when you get to Newquay that you wonder how somewhere like Porth Joke can be so near, and yet so very far away. The beach at Porth Joke has good surf, clean sand, is completely undeveloped and is never packed. Perfect.

Porth Joke won't suit the masses, being all about the simple outdoor pleasures, but once you've camped here, those sweet memories will keep pulling you back for a whole lifetime.

THE UPSIDE: Lovely, small, secluded site near the pounding Atlantic surf.

THE DOWNSIDE: Always full in school holidays.

THE DAMAGE: Pre-booked pitches: adults £55 per person per week, children £30 per week; un-booked pitches £9 per adult and £4.50 per child per night. No infants under 1 year. No dogs.

THE FACILITIES: Decent though not dazzling facilities under the fig trees with toilets, showers and hot and cold water to wash basins.

NEAREST DECENT PUB: The Smugglers Den Inn (01637 830209) at Cubert is a thatched inn with real atmosphere, traditional food and local ales.

Watergate Bay, on the far side of Newquay is home to the much-publicised Fifteen Restaurant (01637 861000) where disadvantaged youngsters are taught the cooking trade.

IF IT RAINS: Go surfing, you're wet already. Take a trip on the quaint Lappa Valley Steam Railway (01872 510317). Or walk through underwater tunnels at the Blue Reef Aquarium (01637 878134) in Newquay.

TREAT YOURSELF: To The Adventure Centre's (01637 872444) answer to bungee jumping – a hair-raising zip wire ride that is one of Europe's longest, highest and fastest.

GETTING THERE: On the A3075 Newquay to Redruth road, take the first minor road right signposted to Crantock. After 2 miles (through Crantock) turn left into a lane to Treago Farm, continue on through the farm (and campsite) through the gate onto a track in the dunes on Cubert Common. The campsite is half a mile along the track.

OPEN: Easter–Oct.

IF IT'S FULL: Go back to Treago Farm (01637 830277) along that bumpy track. Despite it being bigger and further from the beach, it is an excellent site in all respects.

Porth Joke Campsite, Treago Mill, Crantock, Newquay, Cornwall TR8 5QS

	t	01637 830213	w	www.treagomill.co.uk

south penquite

'Diversification' is the buzzword in the farming industry. It's shorthand for 'there's no profit in farming any more, so let's do something else instead'. That's exactly what the Fairmans have done at South Penquite, a 200-acre farm on the edge of Bodmin Moor.

They built a website to promote their attractions: camping, fishing, school field trips and art days. And they transformed the farm: it achieved full organic status in 2001.

The Fairmans care as much about their site as they do their farm. The well-maintained camping fields have restricted numbers so they never get overly busy. The unmarked pitches are huge and there's plenty of room for kids to run around. Solar panels on the pine-clad shower block deliver heated rainwater into four family-sized bathrooms, lined with recycled plastic bottles and yoghurt pots, so you're doing your bit for the environment just by keeping clean!

The innovation doesn't stop there. Three authentic Mongolian yurts sit in an adjacent field. Named Daddy Bear (the largest; sleeps six), Mummy Bear (sleeps four) and Baby Bear (sleeps two), the round-top tents are fully equipped to provide an agreeable balance between 'back to nature' and 'home comforts'.

There is a spiritual quality in the moorland around here; you can almost feel ancient pagan forces at work as the light wind rustles through the trees. If diversification allows us to rediscover such beauty in our countryside, we're all for it.

THE UPSIDE: Mongolian chic on the moor's edge.

THE DOWNSIDE: Short walk from the yurts to the loos; bring your wellies!

THE DAMAGE: Yurts start at £190 per week rising to £320 for the largest yurt in August. Off-peak short breaks are available for half the weekly price. Camping is £5/3 per adult/child.

THE FACILITIES: Good showers and washing-up facilities; yurts come fully equipped, but without bedding. Laundry room with coin-operated washing machines and dryers. Fire wood on sale, and there's a kids' playground.

NEAREST DECENT PUB: As luck would have it, a recent winner of CAMRA's Pub of the Year is within 15 minutes' walking distance. The Blisland Inn (01208 850739) overlooks the village green at Blisland and serves tasty real ales as well as basic basket meals.

FOOD AND DRINK: Sample some of the lamb burgers and sausages from the on-site shop, or venture into the village shop (01209 851730) for local cheeses and, of course, Cornish pasties.

IF IT RAINS: Listen to the rain hammering on the biomes at The Eden Project (01726 811911). Or if you want to venture further afield, head to the Maritime Museum (01326 313388) in Falmouth.

TREAT YOURSELF: To a day in the saddle exploring the moors. Hallagenna Farm (01208 851500) can organise treks and trails.

GETTING THERE: Entering Cornwall on the A30, look out for the right turning signposted to St Breward. Follow this road for about 3 miles until you see the turning for South Penquite on the left.

OPEN: May–Oct.

IF IT'S FULL: At nearby Padstow is the *Cool Camping* site at Dennis Cove (p32).

South Penquite, Blisland, Bodmin, Cornwall PL30 4LH | t | 01208 850491 | w | www.southpenquite.co.uk

bay view farm

The story of Bay View Farm begins way back in 1972. A young Cornish cattle farmer called Mike was in need of a decent bull for his herd. He learned of a strong, sturdy specimen for sale at a farm near Looe and went to have a look. When he arrived, he was bowled over – not by the bull, but by the location. The farm and adjacent camping field were perched on a cliff to the east of Looe commanding outrageous views of the coast and across the sea to nearby St George's Island. The place was overgrown and run down, but that just added to its charm. Mike was smitten.

That evening he returned to his young bride Liz to tell her he hadn't bought the bull, but had found a place he could retire to. She gently reminded him it would be 30 years before they could think about retirement, and not to talk such nonsense. Both the bull and the farm were quickly forgotten.

Fast forward to 1999. The same, slightly older cattle farmer, now sporting grey whiskers, was leafing through the *Cornish Times* newspaper when he happened across the very same farm for sale. The auction guide price was too high, but when it didn't sell under the hammer, he approached the vendors.

Call it fate, good fortune or serendipity, Liz and Mike are now the proud owners of Bay View Farm. You can tell they absolutely adore this place by the passion with which they speak about it and the care and attention that goes into its upkeep. For them, it's not a chore to run this campsite, but an opportunity to share this delightful spot with others.

When you see the view, you realise why. It's about as good as it gets on the south coast of Cornwall, with vistas across to West Looe on the far side of Hanner Fore. You can also see across the water to St George's Island, which has a similar story to that of Bay View – someone fell in love with the place and bought it to retire to, in this case a schoolmistress from Surrey and her sister. Although not the most likely candidates to live on a weather-ravaged and remote island with no running water, electricity or other inhabitants, they threw themselves into life on St George's and lived there for many years until they died. Thankfully, they turned down multi-million pound offers for the island from developers and it has now passed to the Cornwall Wildlife Trust who maintain it as a nature reserve.

Back at Bay View, Mike and Liz keep everything just so, from the brand new amenities block to the prize-winning shire horses in the adjacent field. It's not a large site: there are just 16 pitches available to tents, motorhomes and caravans in the camping field, which tilts at an increasingly steep angle towards the sea. Sleep the wrong way and you'll have blood rushing to your head, sleep the right way and you'll be able to enjoy the view in the morning without getting out of bed.

Nearby attractions include Polperro, a quaint and picturesque fishing village with

tea rooms, fudge shops and galleries in a car-free higgle-piggle of alleys and narrow lanes. You can also find fresh fish for your BBQ, or if cooking sounds too much like hard work, head to the oldy-worldy Three Pilchards pub by the quay for locally caught fish and tasty ales.

Mike and Liz are certainly very happy at Bay View Farm and are happier still when sharing it with guests. So the story has the perfect ending: two happy semi-retirees, a campsite and a field full of shire horses. No bull.

THE UPSIDE: A good base for exploring a less fashionable but interesting part of Cornwall; a panoramic view.

THE DOWNSIDE: Site is exposed so watch the weather.

THE DAMAGE: £10–17.50 per night for a pitch, 2 adults and 2 children. £2.50 for electric hook-up.

THE FACILITIES: Toilets, free hot showers, coin-operated laundry, electric hook-ups and wi-fi.

NEAREST DECENT PUB: In summer, enjoy the views from the beer garden at The Smugglers Inn (01503 250646), Seaton, just 45 metres from the beach. In winter, head for the snug Three Pilchards (01503 272233) in Polperro.

FOOD AND DRINK: Visit Purely Cornish deli (01503 262696) in Looe for supplies from small Cornish producers.

IF IT RAINS: Explore Polperro or the other fishing villages on the coast; the Eden Project is about 10 miles away.

TREAT YOURSELF: To some shark fishing with The Energy of Looe (01503 263747).

GETTING THERE: From Plymouth, take the A38 to Trerulfoot roundabout. From here follow signs for Looe on B3253/A387 until you reach No Man's Land, where you bear left to follow signs for the Monkey Sanctuary and then Bay View Farm.

OPEN: All year.

IF IT'S FULL: The Cool Camping sites at South Penquite (p40) and Dennis Cove (p32) are nearby.

Bay View Farm, St Martins, Looe, Cornwall PL13 1NZ   t   01503 265922   w   www.looebaycaravans.co.uk

slapton sands

At first glance, this campsite, owned and operated by the Camping and Caravanning Club, may not seem to be an obvious *Cool Camping* site. Too normal by far: an organised reception building with efficient friendly staff beavering eagerly away behind computer screens; carefully manicured acres of immaculate grounds; generous metrically measured-out pitches; and superb all-encompassing but predictable facilities. Have we sold it to you yet? No, thought not. Now, let's reveal what makes this place so special – the most stunning panoramic view over Start Bay; only eight caravans can rock up at any one time; the landscaping isn't just the usual gravel, with hedges between; and the atmosphere is relaxed and very much un-club-like.

This pretty site is a busy family camping place (in the school holidays at least) and has a playground for the kids, equipped with all the usual swings and stuff. So, to recap, it's a genuine tenter's campsite, with superb facilities, nice landscaping, a playground to keep the children amused and the view is enchanting. Oh, and with pleasant efficient staff running things there will be no rowdy, sleepless nights

under nylon here. What more can you ask? What more is there? Well, just put your comfiest sandals or shoes on and come for a walk down the lane. Or perhaps up the lane first to the sumptuously quaint village of Slapton, where it looks just like a long-lost rural French *ville* and where the pubs are good, too.

Heading down the hill towards the sea, Slapton Ley is our first encounter – a lagoon that was cut off from the sea many moons ago by the shingle washed up on the beach. The result is a freshwater lake teeming with wildlife that is now a National Nature Reserve. A bit further down the lane is the sea, where Start Bay's miles and miles of unspoilt undeveloped shingle beach stretch to what seems like eternity in both directions. The sea here is relatively sheltered and on calm days the beach is a popular swimming place.

The village of Torcross lies about a mile and a half (the length of the lake, by the way) across Start Bay to the south, where the only real signs of human civilisation are to be seen. There is a pub, a café, a bit of a promenade and an American tank in the car park. The small tank has been here ever since it was rescued from the bay after the Second World War, and it's hard to resist having a good look at it.

Further south Start Bay becomes a wild and wonderful walking place, where the crowds of South Devon thin out to a light scattering. To the north of Start Bay, just a few miles away, you can inspect the delights of Dartmouth or enjoy a delightful boat trip up the river to Totnes. And should your

holiday needs run to mixing with the throngs occasionally, avoid the stress of driving by taking the steam train from Kingswear (which faces Dartmouth across the river) to the chaos of Torbay.

The upshot of all this is that whilst Slapton Sands doesn't score highly for originality, it does rate well for a civilised family holiday in glorious surroundings. And sometimes, that's exactly what you need.

THE UPSIDE: A very well-equipped, well-run site with sea views.

THE DOWNSIDE: A bit too well-organised, if anything.

THE DAMAGE: Adults £5.15–8.60 per night, children £2.35 high season, free in low season. Non-members additional pitch fee is £6 per night.

THE FACILITIES: Excellent modern facilities with toilets, showers, hot and cold water to wash basins, laundry, electric hook-ups and children's playground.

NEAREST DECENT PUB: The Queens Arms (01548 580800) in Slapton village is a traditional

pub with a speciality in real ales; they even hold a Beer Festival in late March. The Tower Inn (01548 580216), again in the village, specialises in seasonal food to a very high standard. Both pubs are within a 5-minute walk of the site.

FOOD AND DRINK: The Real Grub Local Food Centre (01548 581010) provides all manner of local organic food and vegetables. And the Village Shop (01548 580261) in Slapton, in addition to selling the usual supplies, has Internet access.

IF IT RAINS: Get hands on at the Explorocean or just look on and gape at the amazing sealife at the National Marine Aquarium (01752 600301) in Plymouth.

TREAT YOURSELF: To a cruise up the magnificent River Dart to Dartmouth with Riverlink Cruises (01803 834488) or choose another watery route.

GETTING THERE: From A38 take A385 to Totnes, A381 to Kingsbridge, and A379 east through Torcross then left into lane to Slapton following the campsite sign.

OPEN: Easter–end-Oct.

IF IT'S FULL: California Cross Camping and Caravanning Club Site (01548 821297) is another good family site and is situated near Modbury about 17 miles north east of Slapton Sands.

Slapton Sands Camping & Caravanning Club Site, Middle Grounds, Slapton, Kingsbridge, Devon TQ7 2QW				
	t	01548 580538	w	www.campingandcaravanningclub.co.uk

cockingford farm

'I don't want no adverts' snarls the old farmer who runs Cockingford Farm, 'I ain't paying for no adverts'. This was the greeting offered to the *Cool Camping* team on our arrival. The drive to Cockingford Farm, which is situated next to a stream high in the hills of southern Dartmoor, is a nervous, narrow and tortuous thing, and for it to be worthwhile, especially after the frosty reception, this was going to have to be one hell of a good campsite. And it is.

Hidden in one of Dartmoor's deepest crevices, a couple of miles from Widecombe-in-the-Moor, Cockingford Farm is surrounded by some of the finest scenery in southern England. When we visited, the air at Cockingford was alive with the sound of children having fun, which is perhaps the last thing to be expected in such a remote location and on such a basic campsite. But the mixture of stunning scenery and the simple aquatic pleasures of the youngsters on a warm day are the stuff of long-lasting memories. Indeed, a quick poll revealed that most of the adults were here as a result of childhood visits many years ago – and now, to continue the tradition, they bring their own children.

The facilities are quite basic and most of the site lies on a steep-ish slope, but such matters seem of little importance in a location as beautiful as this. As for the less-than-enthusiastic welcome we received, well it could be that he is just a grumpy old farmer, but we prefer to think that the secretive and peaceful nature of Cockingford is more important to the proprietor than a few more customers. We wish him luck.

THE UPSIDE: In a stunningly scenic location and cheap, too.

THE DOWNSIDE: Difficult access and a grumpy owner.

THE DAMAGE: Adults £2.50 each per night, children £1.

THE FACILITIES: Basic, a bit neglected, but do the job. They include toilets, showers and wash basins.

NEAREST DECENT PUB: At Widecombe-in-the-Moor the Old Inn serves well-presented pub-grub, and just about all the food is locally sourced.

FOOD AND DRINK: There is a sign outside the house intimating that home-grown courgettes are for sale, but we didn't dare ask for any further enlightenment or information.

IF IT RAINS: Head for Dartmoor Otters (01364 642916) in nearby Buckfastleigh. These playful and cute creatures will delight people of any age. Plus, they have a butterfly house on the site too.

TREAT YOURSELF: To a day in the saddle on Dartmoor. Shilstone Rocks Riding Centre (01364 621281) can arrange something to suit complete beginners to advanced riders.

GETTING THERE: The most direct approach is to leave the A38 at Ashburton then in the centre of Ashburton turn right into a narrow road to Buckland. Continue through Buckland and after 1 mile turn left (signposted Widecombe; the site is on the left at the bottom of the hill.

OPEN: Mid-Mar–mid-Nov.

IF IT'S FULL: Parkers Farm, near Ashburton (01364 654869) is a large, immaculate and well-equipped site with animals on site and 'walks' around the farm.

Cockingford Farm Campsite, Widecombe-in-the-Moor, Devon TQ13 7TG t 01364 621258

croyde bay

Acres of sand, pounding surf and bronzed lifeguards – welcome to the Gold Coast. Not the original Australian Gold Coast, but the North Devon version; slightly cooler, and more importantly, much nearer for us Poms.

There's no disputing the beauty of Croyde Bay, a wide sweep of dune-backed sand flanked by the finest field-green North Devon hills. It's also the nearest thing you'll find to a fair dinkum Aussie surf beach in this part of the world, although the Australian lifeguards on duty would probably disagree, given the difference in temperature between the two hemispheres. The surf is some of the best in North Devon with the full force of the Atlantic swell providing hollow, low-tide waves and rideable beach breaks. It's serious surf, but this beach is as popular with beginners as experienced surfers thanks to the number of surf shops and surf schools located here.

Along with nearby Woolacombe, Croyde Bay is the venue for North Devon's annual Oceanfest, a freesports and music festival held every year in June, just before Glastonbury. With events including surfing, beach volleyball, kite surfing, skateboarding, BMX jumping and a live music stage, it has grown over the years to become one of the most popular extreme and oceansports events in Europe and helps to give this town its young, lively, surfer-dude atmosphere.

Due to the sheer number of summer visitors, the entire bay seems to turn into one massive campsite during the months of July and August. All the sites are booked up and every spare inch of space is taken by a tent. Many of the campsites in town are small and only open for a month in summer, so we have chosen to mention more than one worthy campsite in the bay.

The pick of the campsites is the small but special Mitchum Meadow, the only site with direct beach views. You can keep an eye on the surf from your tent and run down to the beach when the waves are good. Due to planning restrictions, it's not open all year, but is always open in August. The owner Guy uses another field nearby (Myrtle Meadow) at other times, but it lacks the ocean outlook. Facilities are basic, with spotless shower blocks, but these unfortunately spoil the views from the pitches higher up the field. Despite that, it's a magnificent location where you can fall asleep to the sounds of the crashing waves and dream of being a champion surfer.

Another popular site is Surfer's Paradise, which boasts the nearest position to the beach, just behind the dunes. It's marketed squarely at young surfers and has a reputation for raucous partying so bring ear plugs if you want to sleep at night or an eye mask if you'll be partying all night and sleeping in the day. The site is owned by Ruda, the local campsite conglomerate who also run a giant corporate holiday park in town, where the on-site shopping centre is larger than all the shops in Croyde village combined.

Other campsites include the family-friendly Bay View Farm, which has modern facilities but only takes seven-night bookings in peak periods, and the lovely Cherry Tree Farm set on a hill above the village, which is more spacious and has a friendly and relaxed feel.

Despite the summer influx, Croyde village retains its rural charm with traditional thatched cottages, blooming gardens and a suitably old-fashioned post office and village store. Surprisingly, there's also an abundance of tall, swaying palm trees that seem to flourish in this area. Perhaps it is just like Australia's Gold Coast after all…

THE UPSIDE: Beachside location, great for surfers.

THE DOWNSIDE: Small and squashy site; only small tents accepted.

THE DAMAGE: Prices vary; call for details. No pets, caravans, awnings or frame tents.

THE FACILITIES: Good showers and toilets. Hot water, freezer packs in summer. Late-night opening on Friday nights.

NEAREST DECENT PUB: The Thatch (01271 890349), on the main road through the village, is a lively surfers hang-out with food and a good vibe.

FOOD AND DRINK: Find out more about organic farming and conservation at the dairy at West Hill Farm (01271 815477). And taste their wares.

IF IT RAINS: Surfing doesn't stop when it rains, so don't make excuses – hire boards or organise lessons with Surfing Croyde Bay (01271 891200) or Point Breaks (01271 817422). If you're visiting in June check out www.goldcoastoceanfest.co.uk.

TREAT YOURSELF: To a new surfboard or wet suit at any of the surf shops in town.

GETTING THERE: Croyde is about 8 miles northwest of Barnstaple. Follow the A361 to Braunton, then take the B3231 into Croyde. Turn left in the centre of the village, then left again onto Moor Lane. The village site is just there on the left; the Beach site's is all the way down Moor Lane on the right.

OPEN: Jul & Aug plus other weekends. Call for details about special group bookings.

IF IT'S FULL: Head for Surfer's Paradise (01271 890671; www.surfparadise.co.uk), Bay View Farm (01271 890501; www.bayviewfarm.co.uk) or Cherry Tree Farm (01271 890386).

Mitchum Beach Site and Mitchum Village Site, Moor Lane, Croyde, Devon EX33 1NU

| t | 01271 814022 | w | www.croydebay.co.uk |

lundy island

Lundy Island, a bold outcrop of granite, juts over 120 metres into the air from the Bristol Channel. It's just 11 miles from the North Devon coast, but feels more remote; the landscape is barren and desolate, with wild, towering cliffs, wind-battered fields and little in the way of trees or shelter. With a permanent population of around 20 in summer and a good few less in winter, it's obviously not the most hospitable of places.

Let's be honest, this isn't camping for beginners. In fact, it probably doesn't sound like the place for camping at all! But despite its bleak, isolated location, a few nights in a tent here can be invigorating and truly spectacular. When the wind drops and the sun appears, this may well be England's most magical camping experience.

Lundy is managed by the Landmark Trust, who maintain the island for the benefit of tourists. They operate a ferry service during summer from Ilfracombe and Bideford, and a helicopter service in the winter.

Like all the best natural campsites, Lundy Island's is essentially a field with nothing in it. Its peaceful, remote location feels a million miles away from modern life.

The focal point on the island is The Marisco Tavern. It never shuts, so at any time of day or night, there's always a place to take shelter and swap stories of tents blowing away in the Atlantic winds. Next door, the island shop is amazingly well stocked – apparently, it does a good trade in heavy-duty tent pegs.

THE UPSIDE: Extreme camping on a unique island.

THE DOWNSIDE: Limited water supplies, so a maximum of 40 campers at any one time.

THE DAMAGE: £7–10 per person per night, advance booking essential.

THE FACILITIES: Well-equipped shower block with hot showers and toilets, plus washing machine. The shop and tavern are 2 minutes' walk from the campsite. There's no electricity after midnight so bring a torch.

NEAREST DECENT PUB: The Marisco Tavern is not only the nearest pub but the only pub! Serves tasty food including Lundy lamb and locally caught fish; it's also the place to chat to the islanders or the warden and to check the noticeboard for what's going on.

FOOD AND DRINK: Lundy lamb is famous and delicious. Lambs are reared on their mothers' milk and the grasses and herbs on the island.

IF IT RAINS: Sounds like time for an extended visit to The Marisco Tavern!

TREAT YOURSELF: To a snorkelling safari with the island warden in the summer months.

GETTING THERE: The island ship, MS *Oldenburg*, departs from Bideford and Ilfracombe between March and October (adult/child return £52/26). A helicopter shuttle service runs during the winter (£87/46). Contact the shore office.

OPEN: Apr–Oct.

IF IT'S FULL: There's the great sea-view *Cool Camping* site back on the mainland at Little Meadow (p58).

Lundy Island Campsite, Lundy Shore Office, The Quay, Bideford, Devon EX39 2LY

	t	01271 863636	w	www.lundyisland.co.uk

little meadow

The North Devon coast, designated an Area of Outstanding Natural Beauty, is one of Britain's finest landscapes. It has everything: dramatic granite cliffs, wide, sandy beaches and quaint little coves and harbours. At its eastern edge are the green valleys and vast open spaces of Exmoor; to the west, the picture-perfect fishing village of Clovelly.

With such an interesting diversity of landscape, it's not surprising that huge, commercial holiday parks are common in the area. Thankfully, there is also a small, friendly campsite tucked away here, happily minding its own business. It has one of the best views in North Devon, overlooking Watermouth Bay, the Bristol Channel and the cliffs of Hangman Point.

Little Meadow, a modest, unassuming campsite two miles east of Ilfracombe, relies on its position to pull in the punters without having to resort to water slides, amusement arcades and nightly entertainment. Even so, the owners have worked hard to ensure that everyone can enjoy the views from this hillside location by levelling off the land to create a series of terraces. Dividing the campsite like this also means more privacy; you'd never know there are 50 pitches here. The terraces are perfect for camping, being

plumb-line level with well-tended soft grass for easy tent-pegging. Bright splashes of roses and dianthus border the pitching areas, framing the view with colour. It's a magnificent spot in which to settle comfortably into a deckchair with a cool beer and to survey the scenery. You might even spy a seal or a basking shark if you're lucky and in possession of a good pair of binoculars.

The owners of Little Meadow have created a low-impact, environmentally friendly site and are quite determined that visitors do their bit too – recycling is compulsory and long, wasteful showers are discouraged. It's not a chore to get involved, in fact, the 'can-crusher' is great fun and highly addictive, and if people leave with greater awareness of their environmental responsibilities, then it's worthwhile.

Walkers will love the fact that the longest footpath in Britain, the South West Coast Path, runs right past the campsite. The footpath begins at Minehead and closely follows the North Devon shoreline southwest past Little Meadow, on through Cornwall to Land's End, then back along the south coast through Cornwall, Devon and Dorset, ending up near Poole. It's a magnificent walk and well signposted. The section east of Little Meadow is particularly rewarding as it leads up to the spectacular cliffs of Great Hangman, the highest point on the path at 315 metres. The downside is that it's uphill all the way from Watermouth.

Although you can't see it through the trees from the campsite, the picturesque harbour of Watermouth Cove is directly below. It's a sharp, narrow inlet with a history linked to smuggling, full of small boats at high tide and muddy sand at low tide. Given its proximity to the campsite, it might be worth considering arrival by sea as an alternative means of transport, particularly if the M5 is full of Bank Holiday traffic. Just behind the cove is the solid bulk of 150-year-old Watermouth Castle, now a popular theme park for younger kids. Nearby are the Blue Flag golden sands of Woolacombe, Croyde Bay and Saunton Sands.

The nearest town to the campsite is Ilfracombe, with restaurants, pubs and various tourist diversions including the Landmark Theatre and day trips to nearby Lundy Island (see p56). Apparently, Ilfracombe enjoys some of the highest average year-round temperatures in the UK, confirming that this place really is the coast with the most.

THE UPSIDE: Well-tended terraces providing magnificent ocean views.

THE DOWNSIDE: The hillside position can be exposed and a bit draughty in high winds.

THE DAMAGE: Car, tent and 2 people cost £8–16, depending on the season.

THE FACILITIES: New amenities block with toilets and hot showers, and hairdryers in the ladies block. Gas and ice pack exchange, basic shop on site selling essentials. Electric hook-ups available. Small, wooded play area for kids and wi-fi.

NEAREST DECENT PUB: Within walking distance, The Old Sawmill Inn (01271 882259) is a perfectly serviceable family pub down the hill near Watermouth Bay. Amongst the tack and tat of Ilfracombe, The Quay (01271 868090) stands out for its wide selection of wines, tasty tapas and its chilled-out vibe.

FOOD AND DRINK: The on-site shop sells the unique Lundy lamb (see p57), milk, cheese, eggs and home-made cakes.

IF IT RAINS: There's the Embassy Cinema in Ilfracombe (01271 862323) to while away an afternoon or evening.

TREAT YOURSELF: To some underground exploration at Tunnels Beaches (01271 879882) where hand-carved tunnels lead to sheltered beaches, coves and a tidal swimming pool.

GETTING THERE: Little Meadow lies between Ilfracombe and Combe Martin. It's about an hour from the M5; leave at J27, take the A361 to Barnstaple. Just past the South Molton exit, turn right to Allercross roundabout (signposted Combe Martin). Go through Combe Martin; the campsite is 500 metres past Watermouth Castle on the left.

PUBLIC TRANSPORT: Get to Barnstaple on the train. You'll then need to catch the bus; there's a bus stop at the site's entrance.

OPEN: Apr–Oct.

IF IT'S FULL: Big Meadow (01271 862282) is another decent spot down near the water's edge at Watermouth Cove.

| Little Meadow, Watermouth, Ilfracombe, North Devon EX34 9SJ | t | 01271 866862 | w | www.littlemeadow.co.uk |

cloud farm

Away from the crowds that gravitate towards the popular coast of North Devon, a much quieter side to this county can be found just a short distance inland. Take a drive through Exmoor and the surrounding area, and you'll virtually have the place to yourself. The landscape changes as you move around, from the wild, sweeping open moorland to lush, wooded valleys virtually hidden away from the world. Peace and tranquillity can be found in abundance in quaint villages and hamlets, including the immaculate country village of Brendon, where you'd be lucky to see anyone at all – holidaymakers or residents.

A few miles from Brendon, if you know where to look, you'll find the beautiful Doone Valley, a sharp 'v'-shaped incision through the landscape. This is the home of the 110-acre Cloud Farm, with a campsite, stables and tea rooms hidden amongst tall pines and steep, purple, heather-clad slopes. The owners, Colin and Jill Harman, have succeeded in creating a relaxed, countryside camping environment. There aren't hundreds of rules to obey, there's no minimum stay in the summer, you can pitch wherever you fancy and campfires are allowed. Most of the campsite itself is situated on a long, thin strip of land

alongside the Badgworthy Water river. You can choose a pitch by the babbling brook, or there's another larger field slightly uphill from the river for those who want to spread out.

The farm, at the end of its own road into the valley, is arranged as a small, self-contained hamlet. As well as the old farmhouse, there's a small shop and tea rooms – don't miss out on the cream teas with giant scones almost the size of birthday cakes. The farm stables are home to 32 fine horses, all of which are available for trekking, another good reason to stay at Cloud Farm. This is perfect riding terrain with access to around 11,000 acres of pristine, car-free countryside. Cloud Farm caters for riders of all levels, whether you're after a gentle meander along the lower valley paths or an exhilarating gallop across the moors. Riders are grouped according to experience with small group sizes of between two and six. You can even bring your own horse; stables and grazing are available for the horse that likes to holiday.

Whether you're exploring Exmoor on horseback or on two feet, you're sure to see a rich diversity of wildlife. This area is home to herons, wild red deer and buzzards as well as the more common Exmoor pony, said to be closely related to prehistoric horses. You can certainly cover extra ground on horseback, but the walking around here is equally rewarding and you'll see more of the wildlife as you wander along the well-marked paths. A few days riding or walking, and it's easy to see why the Doone Valley has been designated one of only three 'truly tranquil' places in England by the Council for the Protection of Rural England.

Given the magical scenery of the Doone Valley, it's no wonder it was chosen as the setting for one of the most successful romantic novels of all time. R. D. Blackmore's

Lorna Doone, set in the turbulent time of Monmouth's rebellion in 1685, tells the story of John Ridd, a farmer, who falls in love with the young Lorna Doone and resolves to win her heart and hand. The perennially popular text even mentions Cloud Farm, a claim to fame that still draws Blackmore fans here, although not in any significant number to spoil this area's laid-back charm.

Now, of course, Cloud Farm is featured in an entirely different book, and we can assure you that the beauty of the Doone Valley is strictly non-fiction.

THE UPSIDE: Riverside camping in a hidden valley with on-site horse-riding.

THE DOWNSIDE: Not quite enough facilities for busy periods, so expect to queue.

THE DAMAGE: Camping from £5.50 per adult per night, £4 per child. Horse riding £20 an hour.

THE FACILITIES: Hot showers, toilets (including disabled facilities) and laundry room. Fridge/freezer facilities are available. There's a tea room where you can get breakfast, snacks, lunch and cream teas. The shop sells groceries, wine, beer, camping accessories and logs.

NEAREST DECENT PUB: No outstanding pubs in the immediate area, but the Stag Hunter Hotel in Brendon (two miles away) does the job, and serves everything and chips for £6–£8.

FOOD AND DRINK: For stacks of local produce head to Lynton farmer's market – generally, on the first Saturday of the month. And you can get freshly baked bread on site.

IF IT RAINS: The seaside resort of Minehead is a short drive away as is the medieval village of Dunster with its hill-top castle.

TREAT YOURSELF: To some more of that fresh air and magical scenery. Active Exmoor (01398 324599) can arrange almost anything from fly-fishing to canoeing to mountain biking.

GETTING THERE: From the main A39 Porlock to Lynton road, take the signposted road to Doone Valley and Malmsmead. Turn right at Oare church for Cloud Farm.

OPEN: All year.

IF IT'S FULL: Doone Valley Campsite (01598 741267) in Oare village also has a riverside location.

Cloud Farm, Oare, nr Brendon, Lynton, Devon EX35 6NU			
	t	01598 741234	w	www.doonevalleyholidays.co.uk

greenacres

Greenacres is unashamedly a family campsite. No ifs, buts or maybes – the main aim of Ros and David Harvie is to provide a safe and comfortable environment for young families to enjoy camping. Since they bought an ordinary campsite 12 years ago, they have gradually transformed it into a site dedicated to giving children a taste of outdoor living. To that end the huge 4½-acre field has just 40 pitches around three sides, with the entire central swathe reserved for various activities.

The site is big enough to accommodate several full-size football pitches, so it's no surprise that the central area provides one – complete with goalposts. Some may find the no dogs rule here a bit restrictive but when a site is this committed to providing good, healthy, energetic leisure activities for children then it becomes a necessity. The grass, by the way, is fit for Wembley.

What you won't find at Greenacres is any kind of visual electronic entertainment, so if your requirements include amusement arcades, computer games or anything else of that ilk then Greenacres may not be for you. What they do provide is a host of simple play equipment, including two 'Wendy' houses (but, why no den for the lads?), swings, see-saws, toys and plenty of bikes for hire. A recent addition are two small battery-powered quad-buggies for junior power fiends and apparently they are as popular as they are slow.

Now, just in case an alarming vision of hundreds of crazed children all flying about the place colliding with anything and everything has just popped up in your worry glands, then fear not – for all this hectic stuff is going on in an area free from cars and tents. There is also a carefully controlled, but very wide, selection of books for both the children and the adults – who will have plenty of time for stress-free reading whilst the small darlings are busy exhausting themselves in the middle of the field.

During the school holidays this site is probably not best suited to those quiet, reclusive couples looking for a bit of solitude, but in early September, when the *Cool Camping* operatives arrived, Greenacres was P&Q personified. The facilities are obviously good enough to make family camping comfortable and reflect the slightly old-fashioned but immaculate nature of the site.

If you do get here out of the main season, with some suitable footwear somewhere in your possession, the magnificently moody Somerset Levels lie just beyond the site's gates and are begging to be put to the boot. The famous Glastonbury Tor, Abbey and the hippy centre of Glastonbury itself are about three miles away across the Levels and make a memorable walk from the site.

The small and cute old town of Shepton Mallet is about the same distance but in the opposite direction. The hilly little stroll to reach the town contrasts with the horizontal nature of the amble to Glastonbury. The lovely and wonderfully compact city of Wells is also nearby, and Cheddar and its amazing gorge aren't too far away either. Cheddar itself is well worth a visit just to see for yourself how tacky the tourist industry can get; but it's a good fun family day out from this most family-friendly of campsites.

THE UPSIDE: Spacious, safe and well-equipped place for young families; out of season, it's very quiet for the more mature camper.

THE DOWNSIDE: It does get booked up in school holidays.

THE DAMAGE: Adults £6 and children £2 per night.

THE FACILITIES: Excellent, immaculate if slightly old-fashioned toilet block. The Harvies are proud of the fact that the kind of people who camp here have treated the building so well for so long, and it is now agreeably retro-chic in style. Facilities include toilets, showers, hot and cold water to wash basins, laundry, electric hook-ups and freezer at reception. There are also bikes of all sizes for hire and many toys provided free for the younger campers.

NEAREST DECENT PUB: The Crossway Inn (01749 899000) at North Wootton is the nearest pub (half a mile), and the food is typical pub-grub. The Crown Inn at Pilton (01749 890295) is another mile or so away but offers a cosier pint of local cider along with very decent food.

FOOD AND DRINK: Pilton Manor Vineyard (01749 890325), 2 miles from the site has decent wines (especially the white), tea rooms and 'tastings'.

IF IT RAINS: Head for cover at Wookey Hole Caves (01749 672243) near Wells; there's much more than just underground stalagmites and stalagtites to marvel at.

TREAT YOURSELF: To a hot-air balloon ride and enjoy the landscape up high. Contact Devon and Somerset Balloons (0845 456 4201).

GETTING THERE: Leave Shepton Mallet on the A37 south, in approximately 2 miles take the A361 towards Glastonbury. After 3 miles (go through Pilton) turn right at the international camping site sign. The campsite is on the left about 2 miles after going through North Wootton.

OPEN: Mar–Oct.

IF IT'S FULL: The *Cool Camping* site at Batcombe Vale (p70) lies about 10 miles east of Greenacres.

Greenacres Camping, Barrow Lane, North Wootton, nr Shepton Mallet, Somerset BA4 4HL | t | 01749 890497

batcombe vale

In our ever-hectic world, places like Batcombe Vale become increasingly precious for those fleeting moments of escape from modern life. Once you've settled in Batcombe Vale, the world outside is a completely forgotten place. It's not so much 'cool' camping, as 'totally chilled out and horizontal camping'.

To call this a campsite is probably an offence under the Trade Description Act; for what it is, really, is a slice of heaven dropped into the middle of rural Somerset. Batcombe Vale sits in a valley, and within this intimate, hidden, green fold in the countryside lies a single house (belonging to the owners), a stream, several large ponds (or small lakes even), a host of magnificent trees scattered about the valley floor and about 40 patches of ground where you can pitch a tent.

There are no roads other than the single strip of tarmac that brings you into the private world of Batcombe Vale, and no trace of any other habitation. The first time you enter this secretive place is a deeply memorable occasion, for as the lane reaches the crest of the hill it then drops suddenly onto a view of a veritable Shangri La. And there, far below, in the centre of this glorious scene, is the campsite. It's a truly breathtaking sight, and nothing else intrudes into this idyllic setting.

Some of the pitches are on different levels: some with a glorious view, others surrounded by the lush, tropical-looking vegetation; and one privileged camper can pitch their small tent right by the lake. The largest of these small lakes has three colourful rowing boats tied up on it (or parked nearby), just for the Batcombe campers. Hidden paths snake about amongst the rampant undergrowth in the valley and small jetties jut out into the water – the whole place is a natural wonderland for the sort of children who can amuse themselves in the Great Outdoors.

The campsite facilities are good, but again a certain, and certainly appropriate, outdoor eccentricity runs through them. Whilst younger campers will find adventures aplenty on the lake and in the wooded valley, the soothing atmosphere of Batcombe Vale will be all the entertainment sensible adults will need.

If, in the end, this camping paradise isn't sufficient and you dare step out of this sheltered enclave, there are many genteel distractions and attractions to be discovered. First and foremost is the almost-forgotten art of pedestrianism – moving from one place to another without motorised means. The paths radiate outwards from Batcombe Vale into the lovely green swathes of Somerset's unknown and undisturbed landscape. Within half an hour's drive (if you have to get in an eco-unfriendly vehicle) are historic places like Wells (with its amazing cathedral) and Glastonbury. At the other end of the spectrum, there is the Fleet Air Arm Museum at Yeovilton or in Sparkford there's the Haynes Motor Museum.

There are plenty of things to do nearby, but Batcombe Vale is a whole (and better) world in itself, and apparently many visitors never leave the site once the wheels have come to rest in this Somerset version of Shangri La.

THE UPSIDE: A hauntingly beautiful haven of peace and tranquillity.

THE DOWNSIDE: Having to leave.

THE DAMAGE: Pitch fee including 2 adults is £15 per night, children over 4 years £2.30 per night.

THE FACILITIES: Excellent, eccentric and all under a huge climbing plant, with toilets, showers, hot and cold water to wash basins, laundry, electric hook-ups and freezer. To annoy the fish in the lakes campers must hold a National Rod Licence. Leave 'em in peace is our advice. Breeds and numbers of dogs allowed are restricted, so dog owners must check in advance.

NEAREST DECENT PUB: Take the pleasant 1-mile walk from the site to the 17th-century Three Horseshoe Inn (01749 850359) in Batcombe, with its award-winning restaurant. Another ancient hostelry with good food is The Lamb Inn (01749 850939) in Upton Noble. It also serves local beer, including Batcombe Best.

FOOD AND DRINK: Gilcombe Organic Farm Shop (01749 813710) in Bruton, just 2 miles from the site, is especially noted for its meat and can supply organic packs for the BBQ.

IF IT RAINS: Petrolheads will love the Haynes Motor Museum in Sparkford (01963 440804). And you may be surprised to find yourself spending a whole day, or at least half a day, wandering around at the Fleet Air Arm Museum (01935 840565) in Yeovilton.

TREAT YOURSELF: To an adrenaline burst, abseiling or caving at Cheddar Caves and Gorge (01934 742343).

GETTING THERE: The easiest approach is from Shepton Mallet along the A37. Take the A371 south and then the B3081 for 3 miles until you see the right turn with the international campsite sign. Batcombe Vale campsite is 1 mile further on the left.

OPEN: Easter–end-Sept.

IF IT'S FULL: Head for the *Cool Camping* site at Greenacres (p66), which is about 10 miles from Batcombe.

Batcombe Vale Campsite, Batcombe Vale, Shepton Mallet, Somerset BA4 6BW

| t | 01749 831207 | w | www.batcombevale.co.uk |

stowford manor farm

There are some campsites whose appeal is hard to define; one so simple that it can only be described as one that instils a sense of well-being in the folk who camp there. Stowford Manor Farm is one such site. We can't fathom whether it attracts the kind of people who lend it a relaxed ambience or whether the site itself has mystical powers.

The campsite is a plain and rather rough piece of land, which sits on the River Frome near the Wiltshire/Somerset border. The facilities are good without being anything to write home about, but they are obviously well cared for. The site has a remarkable feel, being overlooked by the assembled old buildings of Stowford Manor Farm, which positively ooze authentic antiquity. This perfect vision of a bygone England has escaped any tasteless tarting up and simply stands there, radiating its dignity and elegance into the camping field. And what a glorious scene of ancient England to greet you every morning, on zipping back the modern nylon?

Another nod to idyllic times of old is the existence, just downstream, of the Farleigh Hungerford Swimming Club – the only surviving river-based swimming club in Britain with some 2000 members. The club was founded in 1933 in the glorious heyday of wild swimming, when jumping into Britain's rivers, lakes and waterfalls was a popular way to cool off in summer. The activity rather fell out of fashion as foreign holidays became the norm and swimming was reserved for hotter climes, but a recent resurgence in wild swimming has been quietly gathering pace in Britain and the swimming club here is as popular as ever. Many of the club's members camp at Stowford Manor Farm on their swimming trips here, which may help to explain the agreeable, olde-worlde feel to the place, as campers try to recapture the essence of a simpler, innocent era; camping out with the family and splashing about in rivers.

After going on at length about the peace and tranquillity that seems to be so deeply embedded into Stowford Manor Farm, it may seem outrageously incongruous that every summer (late July, and when the site closes its gates to 'normal' campers) it becomes the venue for a Folk Music Festival, which attracts thousands of people to this tranquil place. But such is the eccentricity of rural England.

A little further afield, but not so very far, and certainly within cycling distance, is the Georgian magnificence of Bath and the more intimate delights of Bradford-on-Avon. This area lies within a geographically baffling part of England – you're never quite sure whether you're actually in southern England or in the West Country. Southern icons such as Stonehenge and Longleat are easily accessible from here, yet so is the west coast at genteel little Clevedon, where the famous pier provides a nostalgic look at seaside pleasures.

The wildlife corridor of the Kennet and Avon Canal is less than two miles away, and the towpath leads either into rural Wiltshire (the amazing Caen Locks are 10 miles away) or, in the other direction, into the city of Bath. Continuing the watery theme, the great maritime city of Bristol is also within an easy day's pedalling distance – but if it's backwaters you seek, Stowford and its nearby river swimming club will do just fine. Come on in, the water's lovely!

THE UPSIDE: A peaceful site with river swimming, in an unknown but interesting part of England.

THE DOWNSIDE: The ground can get a bit rough after the festival.

THE DAMAGE: A 1-person tent is £8 per night, a 2-person tent £10 and a family tent with occupants £12 per night.

THE FACILITIES: Good facilities in newly revamped but ancient barn, including toilets, showers, with hot and cold water to wash basins. During the day, you can simply stroll to the farmhouse for a lovely cream tea.

NEAREST DECENT PUB: The Hungerford Arms (01225 752411), half a mile on foot from the site is very popular with the locals and swimmers, has a great view out over Farleigh Hungerford Castle and the Frome Valley and, of course, has local beers and ciders. In Corsley, 4 miles up the road, The White Hart (01373 832805) dishes up gastropub nosh at more imaginative prices.

FOOD AND DRINK: White Row Country Foods (01373 830708) in Frome is famous for its high-quality foods and tea room. The nearest genuine farm shop is about 1 mile from Stowford Manor, at Springleaze Farm (01225 720006) where everything is sourced within a radius of 20 miles.

IF IT RAINS: If you're going to get wet then do it in the river at Farleigh Hungerford Swimming Club (01225 752253) a few hundred metres downstream of the site. Or brave the monkeys at Longleat House and Safari Park (01985 844400).

TREAT YOURSELF: To one of the VIP packages at Bath Racecourse (01225 424609), including champagne, canapés, afternoon tea and that all-important member's badge.

GETTING THERE: The site is situated next to the River Frome and directly off the A366, 3 miles west of Trowbridge, near Bath.

OPEN: All year, except during the festival at the end of July.

IF IT'S FULL: Piccadilly Caravan Park (01249 730260) near Lacock is a small, pleasant and well-equipped site about 12 miles north.

Stowford Manor Farm, Wingfield, Trowbridge, Wiltshire BA14 9LH

| | t | 01225 752253 | w | www.stowfordmanorfarm.co.uk |

sea barn farm

As you turn off the main road and head for Sea Barn Farm, through narrow, mostly single-track country roads, shaded with tall trees on either side, it feels like a pioneering journey of discovery in forgotten Dorset. Other than an immaculate church by the roadside near the halfway point, there's nothing here but the dark road shrouded with vegetation. Then, suddenly you've arrived, and the trees disappear to reveal a gorgeous little tenters' campsite, neatly contained by a low stone wall, and with the most fantastic panorama as a backdrop.

The view of Fleet Lagoon, Lyme Bay and the Jurassic Coast can be seen from many of the pitches; others have views of the countryside and some have no view at all, as pitches are arranged across a sequence of small fieldlets with differing outlooks. A friendly, family atmosphere permeates throughout; kids will be in their element with a great playground, use of a swimming pool and an adjacent field full of amiable, prize-winning cattle to admire.

In truth, the laid-back, low-key, undiscovered ambience at Sea Barn Farm is something of an illusion. It's actually part of a larger operation that includes the adjacent campsite and a caravan touring park. Although they're separate from Sea Barn Farm, guests can use their facilities, which include an outdoor heated swimming pool and a bar and clubhouse. So, it's the best of both worlds at Sea Barn Farm – quiet and peaceful camping, with extra entertainment just next door.

THE UPSIDE: Sea views and a good location to explore Dorset.

THE DOWNSIDE: They do pack them in a bit here, so expect to get to know your neighbours quite well. No direct access to the sea for swimming.

THE DAMAGE: Pitch prices per night including 2 adults £10–17, depending on season; extra adults £4–5; extra kids £1–2.50. No caravans. Hooray!

THE FACILITIES: The already good facilities are currently being updated, so expect clean, modern showers and toilets. There's also a laundry, a shop and electric hook-ups available. The bar/clubhouse and swimming pool are open during peak season at adjacent West Fleet Farm.

NEAREST DECENT PUB: The Ilchester Arms (01305 871243) on Market Street in Abbotsbury, 5 miles away, is a handsome 17th-century coaching inn with some comfy leather chairs, open fires and a good selection of beers, including Speckled Hen and Abbot Ale.

FOOD AND DRINK: Bride Valley Farm Shop (01305 871235) also on Market Street in Abbotsbury is the place to head to for good-quality local meats, including the famous Dorset Longhorn beef, plus pâtés, chutneys, bread and cereals.

IF IT RAINS: Get up close to seals, seahorses and starfish at The Sea Life Centre (01202 666900) in Weymouth.

TREAT YOURSELF: To a wreck dive at one of the many shipwrecks off the coast. A dive boat can be chartered through Skin Deep Diving (01305 787372) in Weymouth.

GETTING THERE: Via the A354 from Dorchester to Weymouth, follow signs for Bridport and the B3157. After Chickerell, turn left at the mini roundabout to Fleet. At the top of the hill, after the church, turn left at the crossroads to Sea Barn Farm.

OPEN: Apr–Sept.

IF IT'S FULL: West Fleet Farm (01305 782218), next door, is operated by the same friendly folk.

| **Sea Barn Farm**, Fleet, Weymouth, Dorset DT3 4ED | t | 01305 782218 | w | www.seabarnfarm.co.uk |

eweleaze farm

So significant and intricate is Dorset's Jurassic coastline that it's protected by UNESCO as a World Heritage Site. As such, it's impossible to get permission to build anything along much of its length; hotels are certainly out of the question and there's no road that runs alongside the coast for any distance. So, the best way to enjoy this area is to get your walking boots on and saunter along the South West Coast Path. The stretch of coastline between Durdle Door and Weymouth is particularly rewarding, with hidden bays and beaches, pristine countryside and sweeping views out across the bay to Weymouth and Portland harbour beyond. Partway along this route lies the very special Eweleaze Farm, which, through a combination of fortuitous geography and formidable effort, has become one of the most agreeable places to camp in England.

Arriving at Eweleaze Farm, you might feel like you've stumbled across a very low-key festival, albeit with no stage, no music and no inflated ticket prices. You can see most of the camping area from the high ground of the access road – seven separate fields and 80 acres, busy with the bustling buzz of campers and a fuzz of canvas. Campfires dot the landscape, burning yellow and orange glows into the evening light, gently smoking the air with the promise of late-night round-the-campfire stories. There's an overwhelming sense of shared energy; a community with a purpose – like some kind of cult celebrating the outdoors. But this festival atmosphere is only one of the many things that make Eweleaze a cut above the average campsite.

High on the list is the location. The view from most pitches is of a curve of coast that hangs lazily to the right, meandering round to Weymouth harbour and finishing at the raised lump of land at Portland. Best spots for view-gazing are the Beach field (which gets very busy) and at the back of the Track field (the first field on the right, which usually has bags of space as it's further from the facilities). But whereas many sites in *Cool Camping* can boast views, not many can offer the added luxury of a private beach, accessed directly from the site. This small but adequate bay of shingle with shallow waters for kids to paddle, splash and play is what makes Eweleaze the first choice for care-free family camping. Surely floating on your back in the warm summer waters is the best way to experience the enormity and beauty of this particular World Heritage Site?

It's good to see that the custodians of Eweleaze Farm take their environmental responsibilities seriously. Most of the showers on-site are solar-powered (including four outdoor showers for those particularly brave campers), recycling is actively encouraged with over 50% of the waste being recycled and the fossil-fuel use for the whole season is just 1180 kg/CO_2. To put that in everyday terms, that's less than a quarter of the annual emissions of the average UK household; not a bad output for around 10,000 holiday 'sleeps'. In addition, the food sold at the farm shop is almost exclusively organic (although the portakabin surroundings don't make it quite the idyllic experience you might expect) and the piles of firewood and kindling for campers to use are donated by a local tree surgeon.

There are other small touches, too – bales of hay are available to sit on around your campfire, adding to the organic, countryside feel, and there's a wood-fired pizza stall selling delicious pizzas. But there is one rather large downside – the campsite is open only during August. But, then, like all of life's treats, perhaps it's the rarity that makes it so special.

THE UPSIDE: A spacious campsite with a private beach on one of the most spectacular sections of Britain's coast. And campfires are allowed!

THE DOWNSIDE: Only open in August. Book well in advance to guarantee a pitch.

THE DAMAGE: Week day rates for adults/children are £5/2.50, rising to £7.50/2.50 at weekends.

THE FACILITIES: Eleven showers in total including four outdoor solar-powered showers; this isn't quite enough at peak times, but there are plans to increase capacity. Composting toilets and modern toilets in each field; straw bales available for campfire seating; firewood available.

NEAREST DECENT PUB: The Smugglers Inn (01305 833125) in Osmington is just less than 2 miles along the coast path, a view-tastic 40-minute walk. It has a pleasant family garden but is rammed in summer, so don't expect a quiet pint. Or prompt service. For a sunset beer, seek out the terrace of The Cove House Inn (01305 820895) on Chesil Beach at Portland. It's not exactly Café del Mar, but this no-frills locals pub is a good spot to catch the last of the day's rays.

FOOD AND DRINK: The on-site farm shop (8am–8pm) sells organic meat (some frozen), vegetables and other essentials. The wood-fired pizza van (midday–8pm) is a popular option.

IF IT RAINS: It's only 5 miles to Dorchester, where you'll find museums devoted to terracotta warriors, dinosaurs, teddy bears and even Tutunkhamun.

TREAT YOURSELF: To a sailing course or hire a sailing boat if you're already qualified. SailLaser (0845 337 3214) in Weymouth offer various levels and packages, from £150.

GETTING THERE: From the east, take the A35 towards Dorchester, then the B3390 and A353 to Osmington. After the village, look out for a speed limit sign, and turn left here onto a dirt track to the farm. From the west on the A353, continue through Preston, look out for the speed limit sign just before Osmington, and turn right and keep going down the dirt track.

OPEN: Aug only.

IF IT'S FULL: Down the road, Osmington Mills (01305 832311) is another handy site for the Jurassic Coast, but without views or private beach.

| **Eweleaze Farm**, Osmington Hill, Osmington, Dorset DT3 6ED | t | 01305 833690 | w | www.eweleaze.co.uk |

downshay farm

A trip to Downshay Farm is a little like embarking on a journey back in time. An ancient steam locomotive services the nearest train station to the campsite, huffing and puffing the six miles between Swanage and Norden. It's a fitting way to arrive, aboard a relic from the bygone era of romantic and memorable travel, a time before Orange-jet and Easy everything, when a large part of the thrill of the trip was the journey itself.

From Harman's Cross station, it's a short uphill walk through narrow country lanes where you may not even see a car nor any other sign of modern life, except in peak summer. Birdsong and the wheezy whistle of the retreating train may well be the only other accompaniment to the sound of your footsteps as thick vegetation on either side of the road becomes big green blinkers, shielding the eyes from present-day buildings and directing you on your path to the past.

Turning right into the farm and on past the old stone farmhouse, you'll find the camping field through a rusty, rickety gate. This is no modern, manicured camping field, mainly through virtue of the fact that it isn't very flat. In fact, it's positively sloping in places, so finding a good pitch is key, as is pitching in a direction to ensure a good night's sleep on these challenging gradients.

But sloping campsites are often on higher ground and higher ground often means views, and so we've arrived at the crux of our journey. The views from Downshay Farm stretch out across the Dorset countryside like an age-old landscape painting. A pallet of greens and browns form a patchwork of fields that fold neatly behind one another where the shallow hills meet, and at the centre of this canvas the eye is drawn to Corfe Castle, a medieval ruin that forms a stunning silhouette against the evening sunset-orange sky. The castle's position was partly chosen for the expansive views, giving early warning of an impending attack but, in this day and age, it's Downshay Farm that can claim the better vista, surely one of the most memorable from a sleeping bag.

If ablutions are on your mind after your journey through the ages to Dorset's past, you'll be pleased to know that facilities here are up-to-date. A mixture of modern pre-fab and older-style wooden blocks house enough of everything to go round – just about – and are hidden discreetly in the dip of the hill near the farmhouse. The large tent field offers about 60 unmarked pitches (there is no specific limit – the owner just brings out the 'full' sign when he thinks it's time) and the field is usually left empty in the centre for games of football or frisbee. Even a couple of goals are provided, but that's it in terms of entertainment facilities, other than the view.

Despite the gradient across much of the camping area, flatter pitches can be found on the lower ground, around the edge of the site, but the trade-off will be a lack of views. And if you've journeyed all this way back in time, you should at least make a point of enjoying Dorset's history stretching out before you; the undeveloped hills, the medieval castle, the smoke and toot of the chugging steam train as it snakes through the valley below. The perfect distraction from all the present-day stress and madness.

THE UPSIDE: Stunning views across the Dorset countryside to Corfe Castle.

THE DOWNSIDE: Mostly sloping pitches, but not too troublesome. Open only for school holidays.

THE DAMAGE: Adults £4 per night, children (4–11) £1, over-11s £2, an extra £1/2/3 for small/medium/large tents and another £1 for cars or boats.

THE FACILITIES: Well-maintained showers and toilets. The separate facilities block for caravanners can be used when the site is busy.

NEAREST DECENT PUB: The real ales and ciders at The Square & Compass in Worth Matravers (see p89) are well worth seeking out, as are more castle views from the pleasant garden at The Scott Arms (01929 480270) in Kingston. Both are a 10-minute drive from the site.

FOOD AND DRINK: Dorset cream teas are to be found aplenty in the village of Corfe Castle.

IF IT RAINS: This part of Dorset has a finely tuned tourist infrastructure, with plenty of attractions for everyone, including the Tank Museum, Bovington (01929 405096) and Teddy Bear Museum, Dorchester (01305 266040).

TREAT YOURSELF: To a steam train ride on Swanage Railway (01929 425800) to Corfe Castle. Trains depart regularly from Harmans Cross station, 5 minutes walk from the campsite.

GETTING THERE: From Wareham, take the A351 following signs to Corfe Castle. Continue past the castle on the A351 for 2 miles. At the crossroads at Harmans Cross, turn right into Haycrafts Lane. Continue on this road for ½ mile and look out for the signs on the right.

PUBLIC TRANSPORT: From Wareham train station, catch the local bus, which runs every 2 hours, to Harmans Cross, from where it's a short walk up the hill.

OPEN: For 10 days around Whitsun weekend, then again for school holidays (mid-July–early Sep). A separate caravan field is open Apr–Oct.

IF IT'S FULL: Norden Farm campsite (01929 480098) on the A352 about half a mile from Corfe Castle is a slick operation on a working farm, with a huge, flat camping field backing onto Dorset countryside, and it's all within walking distance of the castle. The *Cool Camping* sites of Burnbake (p90) and Tom's Field (p88) are both nearby.

Downshay Farm, Haycrafts Lane, Swanage, Dorset BH19 3EB

| | t | 01929 480316 | w | www.downshayfarm.co.uk |

tom's field, langton matravers

In an area of rural Dorset called the Isle of Purbeck, which isn't actually an island, it seems appropriate that Tom's Field isn't in fact Tom's. It was at one stage, but Tom has now pitched his tent in that great campsite in the sky, leaving his field to be loved and camped on by younger generations.

If it isn't Tom's, it is at least a field, so that part of the description is accurate. It's rather a nice field, comprising just over four acres of gently rolling soft grass with old stone walling around much of its perimeter. It's divided into a flat lower field, and a slightly more undulating higher field, which is compensated for by the outlook. If you're looking the right way, you can see a long view seaward across Swanage Bay, and on a clear day you might see the Isle of Wight.

With so many attractions around here, it's difficult to know where to start. The pub is probably as good a place as any, and what a pub the Square & Compass in Worth Matravers is. This gem has become an attraction in its own right, with visitors making a special trip to Worth Matravers to taste the ales and pasties, sit by the fire and bang their heads on the low beams.

This stretch of coast – aka the Jurassic Coast – is now a UNESCO World Heritage Site due to the geologically significant rocks that date back more than 100 million years. With that accolade, it has joined the likes of the Great Barrier Reef and the Grand Canyon as one of the wonders of the natural world. Now, Tom would be proud.

THE UPSIDE: Relaxed campsite with views of Swanage Bay and the Isle of Wight.

THE DOWNSIDE: Can be overcrowded at peak times, rendering the shower facilities inadequate. Advance bookings are not generally accepted.

THE DAMAGE: Tent, 2 people plus car £10.

THE FACILITIES: There's a recently installed solar hot water system, refurbed ladies showers, family room with baby changing, washing-up sinks, disabled facilities and a well-stocked shop.

NEAREST DECENT PUB: As well as the quaint Square & Compass (01929 439229) in Worth Matravers (a 5-minute drive or a half-hour walk away), the excellent Scott Arms (01929 480270) in Kingston has a garden and views of Corfe Castle.

FOOD AND DRINK: Stock up on local, organic and fair-trade produce, including bread and eggs, at the on-site shop; bring your own bag.

IF IT RAINS: Pick up the free 'Swanage & Purbeck' guide at the campsite shop for local attractions, or get the car ferry across Poole Harbour to explore Poole and Bournemouth.

TREAT YOURSELF: To a boat trip along the Jurassic Coast from Swanage. Contact Marsh's Boats (01929 427659).

GETTING THERE: Leave the A35 onto the A351 or A352 (depending on direction) and proceed for 11 miles. Turn right onto Haycrafts Lane; after a mile turn left onto the B3069 and after another mile turn right onto Tom's Field Road.

PUBLIC TRANSPORT: Take the train to Wareham and then the bus, which stops at the site.

OPEN: Mar–Oct.

IF IT'S FULL: The *Cool Camping* site at Burnbake (p90) is just 7 miles to the north of here.

Tom's Field, Tom's Field Road, Langton Matravers, Swanage, Dorset BH19 3HN				
	t	01929 427110	w	www.tomsfieldcamping.co.uk

burnbake

Sometimes you arrive at a campsite and it just doesn't feel right. Too crowded, too open, too near the road, perhaps. Other times, you arrive at a new place and instantly know it's *Cool Camping*. And then there are those rare occasions when you arrive at a site and within minutes you know you'd like to pitch a tent and stay all season. Possibly two. Heck, let's just move in permanently.

Burnbake is one of those instant hits, not through anything obvious or especially different, but because many small plus points quietly add up to create a vibe so relaxed and agreeable that visitors often stay longer than an average camping trip and many return on a regular basis.

The least obvious of these small reasons is that there are no caravans, and therefore none of that TV-aerial-satellite-dish paraphernalia that goes with them. Not something that will be greatly missed by the tenters and those in camper vans here. Then, there's the woodland location. Although small areas have been cleared and grassed for easy pitching, most of the site has simply been left as ancient woodland, with some newer tree screening added for extra privacy. A circular driveway circumnavigates the main camping area, linking many of the clearings on which to pitch, but there also other paths to follow, which lead to secret hidden nooks and crannies. There are no designated pitches, so it's all about having a good old nose around to find your own slice of woodland camping heaven.

The facilities can be found in two tasteful wooden huts, neatly tucked away to one side, amongst the trees. They're big, spacious and cleaned regularly, so another tick there. A small kids' play area provides some low-key fun, including that eternal favourite, the swinging tyre. You can keep your plastic play-houses and expensive bikes, a swinging tyre is really all a child needs for days of fun.

The location of the site couldn't be better for exploring the Isle of Purbeck. The beaches at Studland Bay are a short drive and provide miles of sand for running around on. There's also a private road, owned by BP, that links the campsite with the beaches, some four miles along the flat, straight path. Cars are not permitted, but it's perfect for a family cycling excursion. You may encounter one of the infrequent oil tankers rumbling along, but they're limited to 20 mph, so it's safe.

Walkers to the beach will prefer the more scenic 1½-hour heathland route – maps are available on-site.

The village of Corfe Castle is four miles from the site, and the seaside town of Swanage, some six miles away, provides all the '&'s you'd expect for a sunny summer day out: buckets & spades, fish & chips, pay & display…

Back at Burnbake, one of those small things you wouldn't have missed on your way into the site is a bright white, yellow and blue yurt. This is the site café, run by Liz Moody, who sets up shop here throughout the school holidays. It's a cosy, funky little joint with the merest hint of a hippy vibe, and it's just the ticket if you don't want to cook every night. Liz is obviously one of those visitors who took one look at the place and decided to stay. Living long, idyllic summers amongst the trees at Burnbake, who can blame her?

THE UPSIDE: Relaxed vibe at this sylvanian campsite, a cycle ride form Studland Bay.

THE DOWNSIDE: Three minor annoyances: no recycling facilities, no campfires allowed and an additional charge to use the showers.

THE DAMAGE: An adult with tent, car or camper van £7–9 per night, depending on the season; extra adults £2–4 and children (3–16) £1–3. There's an additional £10 charge (£5 booking fee and £5 car pass) for Bank Holiday weekends.

THE FACILITIES: Two large wooden huts house 6 showers each (shower cards cost 30p or 4 for £1), plus a family room, two washing machines (£2) and outside washing-up sinks. A shop is open for a couple of hours each morning and evening, selling camping food and equipment (no alcohol).

NEAREST DECENT PUB: Nothing within walking distance; The Square & Compass and The Scott Arms (p89) are both a short drive. There's a handful of pubs with food in Corfe Castle village.

FOOD AND DRINK: The on-site yurt café is open 9–11am and 6–9pm and serves breakfasts, pizza, vegetarian food and other wholesome options, all at reasonable prices.

IF IT RAINS: The Monkey World Ape Rescue Centre (01929 462537) near Wareham makes for a fun day out. Bring a banana or two.

TREAT YOURSELF: To afternoon tea in the lovely garden at the Manor House Hotel, Studland Bay (01929 450288). This 18th-century property has views out across the bay and towards Old Harry Rocks; rooms are also available, from £93.

GETTING THERE: The site is between Corfe Castle and Studland just off the B3351. From Wareham take the A351 to Corfe Castle, turn left under the castle onto the Studland Road, taking the third left turn, signposted Rempstone. From the Sandbanks Ferry follow the road through Studland, continue towards Corfe Castle and take the turning right on the brow of a hill, signposted Rempstone. From there follow the campsite signs for a mile; Burnbake is on the right.

PUBLIC TRANSPORT: By train or coach to Weymouth, then a taxi to the site (12 minutes).

OPEN: Mar–Sep.

IF IT'S FULL: Norden Farm (p86) is a good alternative, as are the other *Cool Camping* sites at Downshay Farm (p84) and Tom's Field (p88).

Burnbake Campsite, Rempstone, Corfe Castle, Wareham, Dorset BH20 5JH

	t	01929 480570	w	www.burnbake.com

tom's field, fordingbridge

Just minutes from the M27, the motorway gives way to moorland, drivers reduce speed in homage to the grazing gardeners of the New Forest – the wild ponies – and time slows down in step with the traffic. Cue deep exhalation of city congestion and, ventilated by heather-perfumed air, one remarkably swift passage into the wilderness.

Such accessibility from the conurbations of southern England earns the location big accolades. Still, don't expect to hurry through William the Conqueror's former hunting ground; wild horses may have dragged you here, but they're unlikely to budge from the road till they've had their fill.

Tom Charman's grandmother bequeathed her family the pottery and farmhouse adjoining the field. For years, campers would turn up requesting a pitch, encouraging Tom and his cousins to run an honesty site: a sign at the gate would welcome arrivals and contributions were collected each morning.

'Toms Field' now has 50 plots, managed by Tom and his wife Tina. Numbered pitches run parallel to the road, opposite another line of tents that overlook the moors. Here, parents sit outside their ever-expanding canvas constructions looking almost stunned by the sudden onset of relaxation. At the far end, beside a clutch of woody pitches, is The Copse, a favourite with couples.

You can walk for miles on the moors and explore villages by bike or on horseback. At night, campers laze around, barbecuing food. 'Or the more adventurous,' laughs Tina, 'make the 50-yard pilgrimage to the pub'.

THE UPSIDE: Mingling amongst a string of ponies, a drove of donkeys, a leash of deer and a flutter of butterflies.

THE DOWNSIDE: The site only opens for about 28 days a year. Pre-booking is vital.

THE DAMAGE: A pitch costs £5 per night. Adults are £5 and children (4–13) £2.50 per night. Extra tents or gazebos are £2.50. There's a Bank-Holiday surcharge of £1.

THE FACILITIES: Basic single-sex showers, toilets and freezer pack storage. A mobile shop sells breakfast staples. Expect to see new washing-up sinks in 2008. Otherwise, Tina concurs, 'regulars seem to like things staying exactly as they are'.

NEAREST DECENT PUB: The Fighting Cocks (01425 652462) is a hop and a skip away with outdoor seating and piled-high plates of usual to unusual pub fare, such as New Forest faggots and mash and spicy New Orleans jambalaya.

FOOD AND DRINK: Visit New Forest Cider (01425 403589) to sample and buy locally brewed cider or apple juice made ye-olde-worlde way.

IF IT RAINS: Opt for complete H_2O submersion at the New Forest Water Park (01425 656868), which stays open in most weathers. Water-skiing costs from £25 for 15 minutes (minimum age 6).

GETTING THERE: From the M27 take the B3078 3 miles past Fordingbridge. It's half a mile before the Sandy Balls holiday centre, which is signposted from the M27.

PUBLIC TRANSPORT: Many campers disembark with their bikes at Brokenhurst railway station, 15 miles away and cycle to the site.

OPEN: May Bank Holiday and Whitsun weekends then every weekend in Jul–Aug.

IF IT'S FULL: Head towards Ringwood for the Redshoot Camping Park (01425 473789), a family-run affair next to an inn that hosts two annual beer festivals.

Tom's Field, Godshill Pottery, The Ridge, Fordingbridge, Hampshire SP6 2LN

| | t | 07759 474158 | w | www.tomsfield.com |

roundhill

In a land of rules, regulations, road-markings and traffic lights, the New Forest in Hampshire offers, both literally and metaphorically, a breath of fresh air. Meandering roads go where nature tells them, following the lie of the land. The road edges gently disappear into the forest, with not a yellow line or a curbstone in sight. Horses wander freely around this wooded landscape, grazing on the roads if they so choose. They have right of way here; traffic just has to live with it.

There's something quite liberating about this arrangement. It's as if in a very small way, we're acknowledging that nature is the greater force. We're merely humans, visiting for a time, borrowing these natural resources. In the New Forest, instead of dominating nature, we're living alongside it. And it all works very well.

If you can dodge the horses as far as Brockenhurst, you'll find one of the Forestry Commission's most outstanding campsites, Roundhill. Once an airfield, it's now a large expanse of open heathland right in the middle of the forest, with trees and shrubs breaking up this huge area to create smaller, sheltered pockets of land. There are no designated pitches; just drive around for

a while, find an agreeable spot and as long as you're at least six metres away from the nearest tent, it's all yours.

The campsite is well laid out and well organised, so it's worth familiarising yourself with the layout of the park before you claim a particular tent-sized piece of forest. Where you pitch will be a function of your preference for company or solitude, forest or open space and whether you want to walk or drive to the facilities. Everyone is catered for, including those not particularly keen on dogs – there's a sizeable dog-free area at the back of the campsite with some prime pitches amongst the trees. Other places to note include the lakeside area near reception and the adjacent pine woods, both popular locations with regulars.

As with everywhere else in the New Forest, animals have grazing rights here, so expect to see horses, donkeys, cows and even pigs wandering freely around the campsite. For the most part, they keep themselves to themselves, content to watch these strange-looking campers going about their business. If they get wind of your food, however, it's a different story. The donkeys are highly skilled at unzipping tents with their mouths and helping themselves to whatever they can find. Rumour has it they can even open ring-pulls on cans! The trick is never to encourage them by feeding them and always keep food locked in the car rather than in the tent.

Other than the obvious attractions of exploring the New Forest by car, on foot or on horseback (maps and information available at reception), Roundhill is perfectly located for the National Motor Museum at Beaulieu. This fantastic collection of historic vehicles includes the World Record Breakers *Bluebird* and *Golden*

Arrow. Other exhibits include the *James Bond Experience*, where you can see a number of Q's inventions, including the road-boat from *The World Is Not Enough*. Look out for various events here, including a regular farmer's market, where you can buy fresh New Forest produce.

In an area where cars come second to nature and horses rule the road, it's entirely appropriate to see cars relegated to the status of artefacts at a motor museum. The balance of nature has been restored.

THE UPSIDE: Forest camping with added animals.

THE DOWNSIDE: With all those animals, be careful where you tread! A further downside is that up to 2000 people can camp here in peak periods.

THE DAMAGE: From £8.50 to £17 per night for a pitch with 2 people. Additional adults are £3.50–7 and extra kids are £2–3.

THE FACILITIES: Hot and cold water, showers, washing cubicles, toilets and chemical disposal point. At the helpful reception desk you can buy batteries, tent pegs, maps, bread and milk.

NEAREST DECENT PUB: The Filly Inn (01590 623449), back on the main A337 Leamington Road at Setley is 10 minutes in the car. It's an appealing old-style pub with low oak beams, plenty of tankards and brass paraphernalia on the walls plus traditional pub-grub.

FOOD AND DRINK: Check out Simply Poussin (01590 623063) in Brockenhurst. This brasserie is sister restaurant to the Michelin-starred Le Poussin at the Whitley Ridge Hotel but will make a smaller dent in your wallet.

IF IT RAINS: The National Motor Museum (01590 612345) at Beaulieu is open every day.

TREAT YOURSELF: To a 'Sunday special' at Hotel TerraVina (023 8029 3784) in Netley Marsh. Relax for one more day and take advantage of the inclusive dinner, bed and breakfast rate.

GETTING THERE: From the B3055 at Brockenhurst, turn onto the Beaulieu road and head east for 2 miles.

OPEN: Mar–Oct.

IF IT'S FULL: Hollands Wood (0131 314 6505) is another equally impressive Forestry Commission campsite, but closer to the main road.

Roundhill Campsite, Beaulieu Road, Brockenhurst, Hampshire SO42 7QL

| | t | 0845 130 8224 | w | www.forestholidays.co.uk |

grange farm

In the past few years, the Isle of Wight has shaken off its reputation as an island retirement home and adopted a younger, more vibrant image. At the forefront of this is the realisation amongst England's surfing community that the island has some exceptional waves. It's not just surfing either; kite-surfing, paragliding and summer music festivals are also attracting a new crowd.

The Isle of Wight is shaped like a front-on cow's head. At its temple is a town appropriately enough called Cowes. To either side, at the cow's ears, are the towns of Yarmouth and Ryde, both of which have regular ferry services to the mainland. Beneath the ears, the long jaw and chin of the cow is the south coast, home to the island's best surf spots.

Perched on top of tall sea cliffs at the back of the sandy beach at Brighstone is Grange Farm campsite, a flat, grassy field that goes all the way to the edge of the cliff. You'll need a sturdy tent due to the high winds that can blow in here. The reward is a panoramic, uninterrupted view across the ocean, a lungful of unpolluted sea air and an easy scramble down to the beach below.

The site has deliberately been undeveloped. There is a small shop and kids can get to know the farm animals, including Rodney and Delboy, the resident llamas.

But the main attraction of this modest, flat piece of land is its breezy, cliff-top location, ideal for enjoying the winds of change in a new-look Isle of Wight.

THE UPSIDE: Cliff-top pitches with panoramic sea views and easy access to action and adventure.

THE DOWNSIDE: Exposed location, so expect high winds.

THE DAMAGE: Two people, car and tent £12–14 per night.

THE FACILITIES: Free hot showers, flush toilets, washing-up facilities in heated block. The coin-operated bath and family washroom are nice touches. Launderette, hairdryers, phone and drinks machine also on site.

NEAREST DECENT PUB: The Three Bishops (01983 740226) In Brighstone was undergoing a facelift at time of writing so might now be worth checking out, or head for the beer garden at The Blacksmiths Arms (p104).

FOOD AND DRINK: English wine's come a long way. Check out the local vino at Adgestone Vineyard (01983 402503) in Sandown.

IF IT RAINS: Explore the main town of Newport, but as the island claims to have more sunshine than anywhere else in the UK, it shouldn't be a problem!

TREAT YOURSELF: To a visual extravaganza of water, beach, urban, air and land sports at the annual White Air Extreme Sports Festival (www.whiteair.co.uk).

GETTING THERE: From Fishbourne/Cowes follow signs to Newport then Carisbrooke. At Carisbrooke take the A3323 to Shorwell and Brighstone. Just before Brighstone, turn left by the church and follow New Road all the way to the end. Grange Farm is opposite. From Yarmouth, follow signs to Freshwater Bay, then follow the A3055 for 5 miles, looking out for Grange Farm on the right. See p104 for ferry information.

PUBLIC TRANPORT: From Yarmouth/Newport, take bus 7 to Brighstone. Get off at the Three Bishops and walk ¾ mile to the site.

OPEN: Mar–Nov.

IF IT'S FULL: For a cheap, basic surfer's campsite, head to Compton Farm (01983 740215), a working farm in a sheltered valley.

Grange Farm, Brighstone Bay, Isle of Wight PO30 4DA

| | t | 01983 740296 | w | www.brighstonebay.fsnet.co.uk |

vintage vacations

We can only be grateful that the US does everything so much McBigger and McBetter, because without that super-sized can-do attitude, we might never have experienced one of America's best inventions – the slick, stylish Airstream trailer. It's an incredible feat of engineering and a joy to behold, with effortless, curved lines, a sparkle of silver and a spacious, luxurious interior. This is no ordinary caravan – it's style on wheels.

Built from as early as the 1920s, the Airstream really took off with the popularisation of leisure travel during the post-war boom. It soon became the standard for luxury camping: Hollywood stars demanded them on set, and Armstrong and his fellow astronauts even stayed in an Airstream when they returned from their little jaunt to the moon. The publicity helped to establish the brand nationwide, and the Airstream became an American icon.

The early riveted aluminium trailer was replaced by more modern motorhomes from the 1980s, but the sturdy construction and timeless design of the original has led to a renaissance for these classic caravans. They've gradually been appearing in trailer parks and movie sets in the States in recent

years. Perhaps more unexpected is to see ten particularly fine examples in a small field near Newport on the Isle of Wight.

This is the home of Vintage Vacations, brainchild of photographer Frazer Cunningham and stylist Helen Carey. Their love for all things retro compelled them to import initially just two of these beautiful caravans, a 1965 Tradewind and a 1971 Safari. The exteriors were in mint condition but they restored the tired interiors, staying as faithful as possible to the mid-century origins. The result is a perfect blend of holiday comfort and retro chic.

The Tradewind is the original 1960s glamour van, its high-shine aluminium exterior pinging with colourful reflections. You can almost imagine Marlon Brando or James Dean stepping out from the curve-top door, smoking a cigarette and throwing a moody look in your direction. Inside, the 1960s theme continues with yellow-lacquered kitchen cupboards, colourful curtains and rock 'n' roll CDs, as well as retro games including Tiddlywinks and Fuzzy Felt.

Although Helen and Frazer no longer have the 1970s Safari, they have been working hard to realise their dream and now boast a total of 10 trailers, from the 1940s to the 1960s. As you would expect, they have restored all the trailers with their careful attention to detail to reflect each's era.

When you're ready to return to the present day, you'll find the usual holiday diversions at Newport, the island's biggest town, just 10 minutes in the car. You could take in a show at the historic Apollo Theatre, visit the farmer's market on a Friday morning or hang out at the Quay Arts Centre, a thriving gallery, café and live arts venue housed in a former warehouse on the river bank.

Helen and Frazer love life on the Isle of Wight, having moved here from London to concentrate full time on Vintage Vacations. There are currently eight trailers, each comfortably sleeping four people, and two smaller ones that are perfect for couples. At the moment, the trailers are split between two sites until a new site (planned for 2008) is ready for all 10 trailers to settle in their new home. For visitors or larger groups, an additional tent can be hired by the night – retro floral print, of course.

THE UPSIDE: A unique and memorable camping experience in a shiny bubble of fun.

THE DOWNSIDE: It can be hard to get a booking.

THE DAMAGE: From £145 for 2-night mid-week break, from £150 per trailer for a weekend and up to £495 for a week in high season.

THE FACILITIES: Fridge, cooker, toaster, well-equipped kitchen, shower/bath, linen and towels, radio, CD player, hairdryer, Fuzzy Felt, Tiddlywinks. Toilets are in the adjacent farmhouse. An on-site shop is planned for the new site.

NEAREST DECENT PUB: Many options in nearby Newport but for a great view across the island and out to the Solent, head to the beer garden at The Blacksmiths Arms (01983 529263) in Calbourne on the main Newport to Freshwater road. Good Sunday lunches plus guest ales.

FOOD AND DRINK: Order up a special breakfast 'hamper' packed with local goodies (ok, it arrives in a brown paper bag) from the Wight Hamper Company (01983 875535).

IF IT RAINS: Newport has everything including some traditionally tacky holiday favourites – a Waxworks Museum and Waltzing Waters, a water and light spectacular set to music. There are great tea rooms everywhere on the island.

TREAT YOURSELF: To a scenic chug through the countryside on the Isle of Wight Steam Railway (01983 882204).

GETTING THERE: Detailed directions are supplied on confirmation of booking. For ferry information to the Isle of Wight, contact Wight Link (0870 582 7744) or Red Funnel (0870 444 8898).

OPEN: Mar–Oct; week-long bookings only during Jul & Aug.

IF IT'S FULL: Find a date that's free. There's no substitute for these classic caravans!

| **Vintage Vacations** Newport, Isle of Wight | t | 07802 758113 | w | www.vintagevacations.co.uk |

blackberry wood

There's something of the hippie in Tim and Eva, the young owners of Blackberry Wood, and as at all good family-run campsites their personalities are reflected throughout this very special place. Nestled in the foothills of the South Downs, this secluded campsite is almost lost in the native woodland.

Near the entrance to the campsite a small, flat field accommodates an odd assortment of permanent caravans, some of which are available to hire. The centre of the field is a large play area where Tim occasionally lights a big bonfire and maybe a BBQ, a warm focal point of entertainment and sociability for colder evenings.

Behind this field is Blackberry Wood, a rambling straggle of trees and thicket, with a few tentative footpaths criss-crossing through the undergrowth. Campers can choose one of 20 individual clearings dotted around the dense woodland. Each spot has its own unique personality and most have been named by previous occupants, inspired by the character of the location. Some more obviously named hideaways include Fruity in the shade of a crab apple tree, Minty with its gloriously fresh-smelling herbs, Hawthorns and Bramble Hide. A popular spot is Avalon,

a large and beautifully shaded clearing, an oasis of calm in the hotter summer months. Then there are the more eclectically christened Boho, Wobble and Aroha, the latter of which means 'love' in Maori, and has benefited from an authentic Maori blessing. These delightful clearings allow campers to really get amongst nature and, without sounding too hippified, reconnect with the earth.

To the element of earth is added another pagan element – fire. As more and more campsites refuse to allow campfires, it's refreshing to find a place that positively encourages them. There's something quite magical about being able to fall asleep by a crackling fire in your own woodland clearing. It's like having the best room in a hotel – the woodland suite, perhaps. Except here the roaring log fire doesn't need a chimney, and there's no room service. Logs are available at the house.

Whilst we're on the subject of elements, water is important here too – saving water, that is. Environmentally minded Tim displays prominent notices requesting the responsible use of water, and a new wooden facilities block boasts a waterless urinal in addition to solar lighting.

Blackberry Wood is very much alive with nature; the birds are full of song and the bunny rabbits are full of energy. Even the trees that have been felled by the wind and weather continue to grow horizontally, creating a remarkable living sculpture to admire and a crazy playground to scramble about on.

Once you're finished exploring the woods, you can strike out across the South Downs. Well-kept footpaths and bridleways allow miles of country walking uninterrupted by roads or cars. Depending on which direction you go, a 45-minute walk can take you to the village of Ditchling with its museum and tea room; to the superb Jolly Sportsman pub with outstanding food and ambience; or

to the Black Cap viewpoint, a high point on the South Downs Way from where you can see eight miles across the Sussex countryside to the sea. As always, Tim and Eva have thought of everything, and have drawn up maps of the area, marking all the walks, pubs and other attractions.

All in all, this tiny, unpretentious campsite is one of the best in England, due to the simple fact that untouched nature is valued more highly than comfort and commerciality. And that's exactly what a campsite should be about. It also has the four essential elements that make up a truly great site – earth, fire, water and an exceptional local pub.

THE UPSIDE: Back-to-nature woodland camping with a pagan vibe.

THE DOWNSIDE: It gets booked up far in advance.

THE DAMAGE: Charges are £5 per tent plus £5–7 per adult; children (3–12) half adult price. Two-night minimum stay at weekends and 3-night minimum at Bank Holidays.

THE FACILITIES: Hot showers (20p), flush toilets, washing-up facilities and campfire grills. There's also a new shower/toilet block in the woods. Bike hire and logs for sale on site.

NEAREST DECENT PUB: There's a truly great pub within walking distance. The Jolly Sportsman (01273 890400) in East Chillington is fantastically snug and cosy, and serves up a changing menu of gastro delights.

FOOD AND DRINK: Visit the farmer's market on the second Friday of the month at Garden Pride Garden Centre (01273 846844).

IF IT RAINS: It's only 8 miles to Brighton with its Pier and Pandora's box of attractions. For a more chilled out vibe, make for Lewes (5 miles away).

TREAT YOURSELF: To a trip back in time at the fully restored Jill Windmill in Clayton, open Sunday afternoons throughout the summer.

GETTING THERE: From the M23 continue south onto the A23 for 14 miles. Turn left onto the A273 for about a mile, then bear right onto B2112 New Road for 2 miles. Turn right onto the B2116 Lewes Road and turn left onto Streat Lane after 2 miles. You'll see the site signposted on the right.

OPEN: Apr–Sep.

IF IT'S FULL: There's always plenty of room at Southdown Farm (01273 843278) in Hassocks.

Blackberry Wood, Streat Lane, Streat, nr Ditchling, East Sussex BN6 8RS

| | t | 01273 890035 | w | www.blackberrywood.com |

heaven farm

Everyone's looking for their own slice of camping heaven. And for some, they find it in deepest, darkest Sussex.

Heaven Farm is a curious and quaint little place. Its principal summer activity is feeding hungry mouths at The Stable Tea Rooms, as a visit at lunchtime will confirm. The second big draw is the Nature Trail, an award-winning circuit through wooded parkland and alongside streams, where badger sets and foxes' dens are to be found, as well as the odd bouncing wallaby. (These creatures may be indigenous to Sussex, but one suspects not.) Then, there's the Farm Museum, and what this motley collection of mothballed machinery lacks in excitement, it makes up for in extent. Across the path, a converted cart shed has been commandeered as a craft shop and does a roaring trade in pottery, plants and gifts. So, it's all quite a bustle here in summer with these various comings and goings.

Certainly, the campsite seems like an afterthought, last on the list of Heaven Farm's priorities. Which makes it perfect – a spacious, quiet field, cuddled by trees, tucked away in a forgotten corner of the farm. It's unassuming, unpretentious, undersubscribed – and under two hours from London. And with the Bluebell Railway, Ashdown Forest and Sheffield Park Gardens all within reach, it makes for a great weekend break. Heaven? That may be stretching it a bit, but the kids will certainly love it here.

THE UPSIDE: A quiet, low-key camping base for exploring all that Sussex has to offer.

THE DOWNSIDE: It's quite a trek to the loo and the water tap.

THE DAMAGE: £12–14 per night for a tent and 2 adults; plus £1 per child and £2 per extra adult.

THE FACILITIES: The large camping field has room for about 30 pitches around the edge, some pitches are not level; there's also a smaller Camping & Carvanning Club section in a separate flat paddock. There are three well-maintained showers for campers (no showers between 10am and 5pm). There's no lighting on-site, so a torch is essential. Tea rooms are open 10am–5pm.

NEAREST DECENT PUB: The Coach and Horses (01825 740369) in School Lane, Danehill, 2 miles north, is one of those rare finds where the quality of the food is equal to the character of the pub, and both get top marks here. Try local specialities like Ashdown venison or roast pork belly with black pudding and home-made apple sauce.

FOOD & DRINK: There's a well-stocked organic farm shop on-site. Or stock up on home-made marmalades, chutneys and nut-butters all made by the landlady at the Coach and Horses (see NEAREST DECENT PUB).

IF IT RAINS: There's not much indoorsy around here, other than a steam train ride on the Bluebell Railway (01825 720801). If the rain persists, head to Brighton, 19 miles to the south.

TREAT YOURSELF: To Saturday dinner or Sunday lunch, 1920s-style, on board the Golden Arrow Pullman Dining Train (01825 720801) whilst whizzing through the Sussex countryside.

GETTING THERE: Heaven Farm is well signposted off the A275, 3 miles south of Chelwood Gate and 5 miles north of Chailey.

OPEN: May–Oct.

IF IT'S FULL: The Cool Camping sites of St Ives Farm (p112) and Blackberry Wood (p106) are both an easy drive from here.

Heaven Farm, Furners Green, Uckfield, East Sussex TN22 3RG | t | 01825 790226 | w | www.heavenfarm.co.uk

st ives farm

'Three Cheers for Pooh! (*For who?*) For Pooh! (*Why, what did he do?*) I thought you knew…'

Of the many things that the great Winnie the Pooh did and didn't do, the most significant, as far as this little corner of East Sussex goes, is that he chose to spend his entire fictional life around here – hanging out with Tigger, Piglet, Eeyore and Christopher Robin, eating as much honey as he could get his podgy little paws on and playing Poohsticks from the bridge. What's not known is if he ever chose to stay at St Ives Farm, a quiet, idyllic countryside campsite just outside Hartfield, the village where A. A. Milne penned these famous stories.

Hartfield, a one-street hamlet with a tiny village green and ivy-covered pubs, is the centre of Pooh Country. Milne would spend virtually every weekend here, escaping his hectic London life to enjoy the rural landscape, walking in the Ashdown Forest and writing stories and poetry. The old sweetshop where Christopher Robin used to buy 'bulls eyes' survives to this day, re-named as Pooh Corner and now does a roaring trade in cream teas, pots of honey and general 'Pooh-phernalia'. You can also pick up a map that will direct you to all the haunts frequented by the loveable yellow

bear himself, including 100 Acre Wood, Galleon's Leap and Poohsticks Bridge. And whilst there's more than a whiff of commercialism about the place, you can't help but feel it's all just a bit of wholesome fun.

If you can bear to drag yourself away from all this nostalgic childishness, St Ives Farm is to be found just a five-minute drive north of Hartfield. After following signs for St Ives Tea Rooms, you'll need to take a last minute diversion across a farmer's field and circumnavigate some long-stay caravans before finding the small camping area, offering about 20 tent pitches beside a picturesque fishing lake and surrounded by arable farmland. Be warned, with a limited number of spaces, it's usually booked out by regulars at weekends, so a midweek break may be the only realistic option in summer.

Being so far from the road, St Ives has an unusually peaceful ambience, an atmosphere enhanced by the fact that campfires are allowed and which scent the air with the fragrant smoke of sizzling sausages and melting marshmallows. The car count can also be lower than you might expect, as campers sometimes arrive on foot, weary and worn from a walk on the Weald Way, which runs next to the site. Westwards, the path heads into the Ashdown Forest, and in the other direction a walk to Hartfield will take around 25 minutes.

The only activity on-site is coarse fishing for carp and perch in the well-stocked pond. However, the St Ives Tea Rooms at the farm next door seems to have an impregnable power over visitors to this place, who gravitate helplessly towards the flower-filled tea gardens for scones and jam at least once in their trip; for those fond of jam, once a day. And the news that they also stock pots of honey might attract a certain kind of local bear...

So, it's three cheers for Pooh and for St Ives Farm, too. (*Why, what did they do?*) I thought you knew...

THE UPSIDE: Secluded, lakeside, countryside setting with the added bonus of campfires. Come during the week and have the place to yourselves.

THE DOWNSIDE: Some noise from the planes overhead, but it's not too obtrusive. Weekends are usually booked out.

THE DAMAGE: £14 per night for a family tent, £8 per night for a 2-person tent.

THE FACILITIES: The basic facilities suit this rustic place; just three chemical loos and two showers. Fishing in the lake, stocked with carp and perch, costs £9/5 per day for adults/children.

NEAREST DECENT PUB: The ivy-covered Anchor Inn (01892 770424) in Hartfield is a 15th-century free house with an unusual, old-fashioned, flower-filled veranda, as well as a pleasant beer garden and a selection of local ales.

FOOD AND DRINK: For top-notch food, with an emphasis on locally sourced, seasonal produce head for The Hatch Inn (01342 822363) at Colemans Hatch. It's a quaint little country pub on the edge of Ashdown Forest, a 50-minute walk or 10-minute drive from St Ives Farm and handy for Poohsticks Bridge. French and traditional British influences feature on a changing, innovative menu served in a snug restaurant or in the beer garden.

IF IT RAINS: Go walking with llamas (no, really, it's true) at the Ashdown Forest Llama Park (01825 712040) in Forest Row. One llama each is £30; 2 people sharing a llama is £50. Bizarre!

TREAT YOURSELF: To a pot of honey. Widely available in the area.

GETTING THERE: Take the B2026 north from Hartfield village. Take the first turning left on to Butcherfield Lane and continue for 1½ miles. Take the next left following camping signs, then divert across the field when prompted.

OPEN: Apr–Oct.

IF IT'S FULL: The *Cool Camping* site of Heaven Farm (p110) is only about 10 miles south of here.

| **St Ives Farm**, Butcherfield Lane, Hartfield, East Sussex TN7 4JX | t | 01892 770213 |

sussex tipis

Camping may be cool but there is no denying it can sometimes be a little challenging. If your last memory of camping was of lugging a tent around a muddy field in search of the perfect spot or of tossing and turning through the night tormented by the lumps and bumps beneath you, then perhaps it's time to commune with Mother Nature but with a few additional creature comforts – all within the wondrous confines of your very own tipi.

Set in ten acres of 'hobby' vineyards and lush orchards on the Weald, an Area of Outstanding Natural Beauty just eight miles from the ancient town of Rye, Sussex Tipis offers hassle-free camping. There is no better way to camp, without compromising on comfort and snugness.

Owned and managed by former fashion designer Helen Robinson and her partner Alan House, the vibe here is authentically boho but not in a self-conscious, trendy way. These tipis are almost flawless, although the odd spot of mould on the tipis' canvas exteriors almost certainly can't be helped. But they are probably the nearest you will get to a 'boutique' tent for the price.

Helen and Alan have lovingly furnished each of the six tipis with everything you might need, which means you can start to unwind,

pretty much from the outset. You will find mattresses, cushions, Mexican blankets, sheepskin rugs, a coffee table and a trunk full of cooking utensils, plates, cups and cutlery. Outside there is a wheelbarrow full of chopped wood, a fire ring, five or so stools fashioned out of tree stumps, a kettle and a gas stove for cooking. The only things you will need to bring are a sleeping bag or a duvet, a towel, a torch and some food. Bring some booze, too. Despite the ubiquitous vines, there is no actual wine production as yet.

Helen says she fell in love with the idea of tipis as a child. Setting up the site was a lifelong dream fulfilled, and her obvious enthusiasm for both this idyllic patch of land and the tipis themselves is infectious. The best thing about them, she believes, is their circularity – so very conducive to relaxing and a good old chinwag. And the fire is a great telly substitute.

The 5.5-metre tipis are striking against a cobalt blue sky. The specially treated canvas hails from America but Helen and Alan had to find all the wood (from Sculdown Vineyard pine trees) for the poles and cut each to size. Keeping out the rain can be a challenge because here it falls hard and directly down; whereas in the American plains, it falls across and hits the side of the canvas. So, an extra canvas canopy keeps you and your belongings dry in the event of a downpour.

Surrounded by lush fields and paddocks, home to the odd badger and fox, bees (in beehives), horses and their foals, the tipis are spaced far enough apart to give you and your companions privacy. But, if you wanted to come with a group of friends and take over two or three tipis at once, they are close enough together to create a temporary community for a chilled-out gathering.

When the inevitable urge to go for a wander strikes, there are lovely walks opposite the campsite in Powdermill Wood, or you can take a ride on the Kent and East Sussex Railway line that connects the 'Jewels Of The Weald',

aka Tenterden Town and Bodiam Castle, brushing past the quiet Sussex village of Northiam on the way.

Nearby Rye, with its cobbled streets, 12th-century church and medieval castle is well worth a visit. A snooper's paradise, here you will find an excellent bookshop, junk and charity shops and several antiques shops filled with retro treasures. And nature lovers and wildlife enthusiasts will doubtless be drawn to the wide open spaces of nearby Winchelsea Beach and Camber Sands.

However you fill your time, your tipi will be somewhere warm and welcoming to rest your head come sundown. Even designer tents will never match the simple wonder of tipis.

THE UPSIDE: A feast of orchard fruits – plums, apples and pears – on your doorstep.

THE DOWNSIDE: Tipis don't come cheap.

THE DAMAGE: From £180 for a 2-person tipi for 2 nights to £495 for a 4-person tipi for 7 nights. Or, bring a tent for just £8 per person per night.

THE FACILITIES: The site has hot showers, flushing toilets and washing-up facilities. There is a pub and local store in the village, and a farm shop and supermarkets nearby.

NEAREST DECENT PUB: The Plough in Cock Marling is about 3 miles down the road (that's the B2089). This 400-year-old pub with a garden serves locally sourced and home-made, traditional pub-grub. They also have a decent selection of wine and real ales.

FOOD AND DRINK: Visit the artisan fishery of Botterell's (01797 222875) in Rye. They fish for shrimps on Camber Sands but can also supply sardines, haddock and crab.

IF IT RAINS: Snuggle up inside your tipi and read a book.

TREAT YOURSELF: To dinner at chic boutique hotel and restaurant, The George In Rye (01797 222114). The head chef used to work at Moro in London and food is, as you would expect, imaginative, full of flavour and a little pricey.

GETTING THERE: Take the A21 South towards Hastings. Three miles past Robertsbridge take the B2089 left to Broad Oak. Sculdown Vineyard is 4 miles on the left.

PUBLIC TRANSPORT: Trains for Robertsbridge and Hastings leave from Charing Cross or London Bridge. If you travel by train, you can arrange for owners Helen and Alan to pick you up from Robertsbridge Station. If you arrive on your bike they will offer you a 10% discount.

OPEN: May–Sep.

IF IT'S FULL: Normanhurst Court, Stevens Crouch, Battle (01424 773808) is a far larger campsite, though no less lovely, with views and woodland.

Sussex Tipi Holidays, Sculdown Vineyard, Chitcombe Road, Broad Oak, nr Rye, East Sussex TN31 6EX

| | t | 01424 713 868 | w | www.sussextipiholidays.co.uk |

livingstone lodge

Dawn. A misty sun rises over the marsh. The good morning 'roar' of an ex-Zimbabwean game ranger signals coffee and time to get up – a call from the wild that is the start of your extraordinary journey across the teaming plains of this out-of-Africa experience.

Overlooking the Romney Marshes along the Kentish coast is the 100-acre Port Lympne Wild Animal Park, home to the biggest family of silverback gorillas this side of the Congolese lowlands. John Aspinall, a once notorious gambler and wildlife enthusiast, won the park in a card game and then, flying in the face of sceptism faster than a cheetah on the run, stocked the place with his favourite Indian and African wildlife. His theory – give animals enough space and a close proximity to their natural patch and they will breed. His proof – restocking the Gobi Desert with the once-extinct wild horses from his park.

What the park trust is trying to do in terms of breeding is ambitious. You can't help but gulp when you learn that of the 60,000 black rhino that used to roam the African continent fewer than 3000 are left. And, what's more, the largest breeding herd outside of their home territory is right here at Port Lympne. The stats are impressive. The proud game ranger will reveal that 29 rhinos have been born in the park and at least five rhinos have been sent back to the wild.

En route to your luxury pit stop for the night, you rock and roll through the park in a beast of an open-sided 4x4. On the way you meet Ernie the eland, Daphne the deer and, to top it all, Sebastian the giraffe who, if you're unlucky, might deposit a two-metre-long dollop of dribble in your lap when he pops in to say hello. Luckily, though, giraffe gob does come out in the wash! Taking anything seriously after this is tricky, but hang in there and learn some delightful morsels about the animal kingdom. Like the elephants who are so big, they'd crush their internal organs if they were to lie down, so they sleepwalk instead. A sleepwalking elephant? Definitely something to be avoided.

The lodge itself – a replica of the swish tented camps of Africa – has been up and running since the summer of 2007. Nine enormous luxury canvas tents sit on stilts, perched atop a hill, overlooking vast expanses of marshy countryside and the English Channel. Each heated tent is kitted out with a bed, sumptuous feather duvet and fluffy white gown. There's even a cupboard to hang up clothes and a writing desk should you wish to pen a letter home. More like a hotel than a camp; all that's missing is the directory list for room service. You're not the only ones with a cosy place for the night, the animals also have centrally heated houses for when temperatures plummet below 8°C, which let's face it generally happens a lot more in England than on the African plains!

Once you're settled in, join the other guests for pre-dinner drinks in the Lapa – a canvas lounge with rustic reed furniture and open fire. You can chat or watch hungrily whilst a bonafide South African chef prepares a traditional southern hemisphere feast.

Unlike in Africa where you eat what you've seen that day: kudu steaks and springbok stew; here, you scoff down locally reared fillet beef and locally fished king prawns. Once you're fuller than the four-stomached buffalo you spotted earlier, it's off to bed in anticipation of that pre-dawn call of the lesser-spotted African game ranger.

This misty marshland may be as far away from the dusty Savannah plains as you can get, but it's still a breathtaking experience to share the breaking dawn with these 'wild' animals.

THE UPSIDE: Watching waterhole wildlife behind a heated tent flap, hands round a hot cuppa.

THE DOWNSIDE: Damage to your wallet and English weather dampening the African feel.

THE DAMAGE: £150 per person per night sharing, kids age 9–13 sharing £80; no kids under 9 allowed. Includes a three-course dinner and breakfast.

THE FACILITIES: Nine double, luxury safari tents complete with heating, carpets, beds, duvets and fluffy gowns. Separate shower block with toilets (also disabled) and basins. Communal canvas-covered lounge with fire pit, aka the 'lapa'.

NEAREST DECENT PUB: The experience stays on site with an inclusive buffet dinner of beef fillet, grilled prawns and death by chocolate for pud. Drinks are additional.

IF IT RAINS: You'll still do the drive round in a covered Land Rover, although the animals might head for shelter.

TREAT YOURSELF: To a gin & tonic; it's what you'd be drinking on safari, so why not?

GETTING THERE: Leave M20 at Junction 11 and follow brown tourist signs to the park. There is a separate Lodge check-in entrance, watch for signs from the main entrance of park.

PUBLIC TRANSPORT: Buses serve the railway from Ashford, Canterbury, Folkestone and Dover. Stagecoach East Kent 10 bus runs between Ashford and Folkestone via the park. For times call 01233 620342.

OPEN: June–Sep (Wed–Sun).

IF IT'S FULL: There's nothing else like it, so change your dates!

Livingstone Safari Lodge, Port Lympne Wild Animal Park, Lympne, nr Hythe, Kent CT21 4PD			
	t	01303 234190	w	www.totallywild.net

the warren

The soaring white cliffs of Folkestone and nearby Dover are iconic; a symbol of England's grand coastline and a natural defence against the wild sea and invading troops. They're often the last thing travellers see when leaving England and the first, welcoming sight on returning home. The cliffs have witnessed it all – wars, crazy cross-Channel attempts and underwater tunnels – and through it all, they have stood firm and strong; a reliable constant in a changing world.

Thankfully, no hotels or other buildings are permitted along this cliff edge, but there is one spectacular location, just east of Folkestone, where you can pitch your own room with a view at the foot of the cliffs.

The Warren, operated by the Camping and Caravanning Club, is perhaps their best-located site in England. Set in a particularly attractive curve of the Kentish coast, it has an outlook of Channel waters and chalky crags. It's also one of the closest spots to continental Europe, which makes it handy for a ferry or Channel Tunnel excursion. It's said that you can even see France from your tent on a clear day.

The main camping field is a pristine strip of grass with flat, marked pitches. Those at the end nearest reception are more exposed and have direct views across the Channel. At the furthest end there's more shelter, but at the expense of the sea views. There are also a few special hideaways – tiny little pitches tucked away amongst the trees for just one or two tents – including the secluded Honeymoon pitch.

The facilities at the site are good. There are two well-equipped shower blocks with four showers in each, just enough for this smallish campsite. There's also a family room, disabled facilities and a laundry. There's no shop as such, but you can buy ice creams and other essentials at reception and order newspapers for the morning. Unfortunately, they don't deliver them to the tents…

A path leads down from the campsite to the shingle and sand beach below. Next to this, an odd-looking concrete platform spoils the natural order somewhat. It was originally built to protect the cliffs from further erosion, but now provides a good spot for fishing or for kids to explore the rock-pool-like puddles left behind by the retreating waves. On the far side of the platform, a sandy beach spreads out along the base of the cliffs.

Whereas the white cliffs here are long-lasting symbols of England's grand

heritage, the nearby nature reserve of
Samphire Hoe, between Folkestone and
Dover, is the very newest part of England.
When the Channel Tunnel was built,
millions of tonnes of excavated earth had
to find a new home, so it was decided to
extend England into the sea. The chalk marl
was dumped at the foot of the Shakespeare
Cliff, reclaiming the land and creating this
nature reserve, an intriguing other-world
landscape of chalky earth, salt-water pools,
fescue grasses and wild flowers. The reserve
attracts an incredible diversity of plants,
birds and other wildlife, including the
human variety: walkers, picnickers and
sea-anglers all use this peaceful place to
enjoy the magnificence of the cliffs.

You can walk right along the cliffs from
The Warren to Dover, a good day's walk at a
healthy pace. For a shorter stroll on the
most stunning section, head to Langdon
Cliffs, east of Dover, where an interesting
Visitor Centre explains how these cliffs
were formed. The melting ice caps that
covered Northern Europe more than half a
million years ago forced their way through
the land mass, splitting England from
France, creating the English Channel, these
mighty cliffs and, in the process, one of
England's best camping spots.

THE UPSIDE: White-cliff coastal camping. Handy stopover for trips to France.

THE DOWNSIDE: Exposed pitches in windy weather; long walk to the pub.

THE DAMAGE: Low-season prices per night are £5.15/£2.55 for an adult/child; high season £8.60/£2.35. There's a non-member site fee of £6. Tents and motorhomes only.

THE FACILITIES: Toilets (disabled facilities), showers, family shower room, washing-up sinks, laundry, freezer and chemical disposal point.

NEAREST DECENT PUB: It's a 45-minute walk into Folkestone, and the pubs there aren't much cop. Ask at the site for directions to The Lighthouse (01303 223300) in Capel-le-Ferne where you can enjoy a pint of Ramsgate No 5 and views out across the sea.

FOOD AND DRINK: Go grab yourself some local fresh lobster, mackerel or prawns from one of the fish stalls down in Folkestone harbour.

IF IT RAINS: Dover Castle (01304 211067), an impenetrable fortress overlooking the town, is well worth a day trip.

TREAT YOURSELF: To lunch in France. Pop across the Channel for the day. The Eurotunnel (08705 353535) terminal is the exit before Folkestone, about 15–20 minutes away.

GETTING THERE: From the M20 J13, take the A20 towards Dover for a short way until it crosses the A260. Follow the A260 towards Folkestone, then turn left onto Hill Road, following signs for 'Country Park'. At the junction of Dover Road, turn left then immediately right, onto Wear Bay Rd. Take the second turning on the left and follow the track for half a mile to find The Warren.

PUBLIC TRANSPORT: From Folkestone train station you can catch a bus to within a 10–15-minute walk of the site.

OPEN: Apr–Oct.

IF IT'S FULL: Also accessed from Wear Bay Road is Little Switzerland Campsite (01303 252168). Its pitches are set in beautiful alpine-like scenery.

The Warren, Wear Bay Road, Folkestone, Kent CT19 6NQ

| | t | 01303 255093 | w | www.campingandcaravanningclub.co.uk |

debden house

If you go down to Essex today you're in for a big surprise. Famous for chavs and WAGs, it's also home to Epping Forest, 6000 acres of magnificent ancient trees, flower-carpeted meadows, mirrored ponds and an abundance of wildlife, all on the outskirts of the capital.

Backing directly onto the forest is Debden House's 50-acre campsite, which despite its expanse, pulls off a unique conjuring trick: balancing size with privacy. Towering trees carve the land into seven fields, separating you from the rest of the campsite's sprawl.

Field 1 opens out from the former farmhouse onto a large expanse dotted mainly with camper vans and a kids' play area. Walk on to Field 2 to uncover a surprisingly not-too-often-colonised, secluded patch. A gap in the hedgerow merely hints at its existence. You can sandwich yourself on a narrow strip enclosed by the forest on either side whilst energetic bunnies speed around your tent, here it feels more like back-of-beyond camping than pitching up on a campsite. Large groups (20-plus) are given their own stretches of land in Fields 3 and 7 keeping the noise down for everyone else.

Adding to the rustic camping feel are the two Fire fields. Debden House, refreshingly, gives over Fields 5 and 6 to fans of the flame. In all, 58 pits are available and the logs are free, courtesy of the Forestry Commission.

However, those after a more authentic camping experience can go hunter-gathering to collect their own wood in the forest. Ancient forest by-laws permit commoners 'one faggots worth of dead or downed wood each day' – that's a bundle to you and me in ye olde English. But, the secret is out, so if you lust for fire-side camping, book at least a week in advance as spaces can be thin on the ground come the weekend.

Despite these beguiling rustic charms, a solitary facilities block located at the campsite's entrance in Field 1 means it can be a long, dark, lonely walk at night to find the bathroom. Temporary portaloos are dotted around, though, if you need relief with a festival flavour. The block is also due an overhaul but there are free hot showers, and new blocks are on the drawing board for the near future.

Epping Forest encircles the whole site here – it's a joy to be this close to London, and yet be amongst all this woodland, with the flurry of birdsong to wake you each morning. Footpaths lead off from the camp's edges taking you deep into the heart of the forest, and link up with various other walking paths. Within the forest itself you'll find a menagerie of English wildlife, including deer, rabbits, adders, hawks, kites, foxes and buzzards; many of which roam around or circle above the campsite.

If all that nature gets too much, then you can see how the Royals used to enjoy the forest at Queen Elizabeth's Hunting Lodge, the only timber-framed building left standing in England. Built in 1543 by the medieval womaniser Henry VIII for staging deer hunts, it's said he could often be seen taking pot-shots at the unsuspecting wildlife with his crossbow from the lodge's windows.

Thankfully the deer are protected now, and the kids can get a Bambi fix at the forest's deer sanctuary, a 10-minute stroll from the campsite through the woods; the camp office will gladly put a map in your hand and point you in the right direction.

Whether you seek a country escape from city madness or an alternative rural base to go exploring the capital, this site is ideal: Theydon Bois tube station is just a mile away, whisking you in and out of London's heart along the Central Line within the hour. Debden House really can give you the best of both worlds.

THE UPSIDE: Fire-side camping in a forest setting, just a tube ride from London.

THE DOWNSIDE: Weekends are busy, and the facilities block looks a little tired. There's some noise from the motorway and planes overhead. But, hey, this is London (well, almost)! What do you expect?

THE DAMAGE: £7 per adult per night and £3.50 for children. There's also a family ticket costing £25 for 2 adults and 4 children. Electric hook-ups £3.50 per night. Book in advance for weekends.

THE FACILITIES: Free hot showers, washing-up area, plus a laundry facility and two kids' play areas. The on-site café serves hot and cold meals. Shop on site, but only for food essentials. Don't rely on it for camping equipment. Free

firewood – for fire-side camping you'll also have to follow the somewhat bureaucratic condition of producing a photo ID and a recent utility bill.

NEAREST DECENT PUB: No absolute knockouts, but escape standard pub fare at the 16 String Jacks (01992 813182). A small, friendly, local haunt that's just a 10-minute walk through the forest. It serves home-made food with independently brewed Hertfordshire ales on tap.

FOOD AND DRINK: Check out the farmer's market on the first Sunday of the month.

IF IT RAINS: If you want to stay local rather than whizzing up to London town, then grab some national heritage at Queen Elizabeth's Hunting Lodge (020 8529 6681/020 8529 7090) or head to Waltham Abbey (01992 767897).

TREAT YOURSELF: To afternoon tea at The Wolseley (020 7499 6996) in Piccadilly.

GETTING THERE: Leave the M11 at junction 5 and follow the A1168 toward Loughton. Turn right onto Pyrles Lane, right into Englands Road and follow the brown campsite signs turning left into Debden Road.

PUBLIC TRANSPORT: From London, take the Central Line to Theydon Bois tube station, then catch bus 167 or 20 to the site.

OPEN: May–Sep.

IF IT'S FULL: Elms Caravan and Camping Park (020 8502 5652) in nearby High Beech will do the job for a night, but it's more for caravanners.

| **Debden House**, Debden Green, Loughton, Essex IG10 2NZ | t | 020 8508 3008 | w | www.debdenhouse.com |

clippesby hall

For a campsite of this size and with such extensive facilities, Clippesby Hall near Great Yarmouth in Norfolk, has managed the near-impossible. Despite its large extent, it feels friendly, non-commercial and, above all, very homely.

Clippesby Hall is like its own little self-contained village. Set in the manicured grounds of a small, odd-looking manor house, the campsite has everything you could possibly want and more besides. With 100 pitches (many with electric hook-up), an outdoor swimming pool, grass tennis courts, mini-golf, self-catering cottages, pine lodges and its own family pub, you might assume that this place is about as quiet and peaceful as a night on the hard shoulder of the A12. Well, you'd be wrong. Somehow the owner, John Lindsay, has managed to incorporate all those facilities into the grounds of his family home, whilst still retaining its unique character and personality. The result is an exceptionally tasteful camping park with a relaxed, family atmosphere.

The camping pitches are spread across various areas, each landscaped and spacious enough to avoid any feeling of overcrowding. Each pitch is named according to its individual character: Pine Woods is almost entirely surrounded by conifers, The Orchard has plenty of tree cover amongst the pitches whilst The Dell is hidden away in a quiet corner. Rabbits Grove is a favourite amongst younger campers with bunny rabbits bouncing around. These well laid-out, mid-sized clearings mean that even in busy periods, you can still find a relatively secluded space to call your own.

Clippesby Hall is in a perfect location to explore the Broads National Park, a network of rivers and lakes that forms Britain's largest protected wetland. Although the rivers are natural, the lakes are man-made, the result of 200 years of enthusiastic peat digging from the 12th century onwards. Hundreds of acres of peat were dug up for fuel in the absence of suitable woodland in the area. However, water soon began seeping through the porous ground, causing marshes and then lakes to appear. In a centuries-old example of how human intervention can significantly change the landscape, nature has also demonstrated its resilience to adapt to a changing environment, and this collaboration of industry and nature has resulted in a stunning waterscape.

A good place to start exploring the Broads is the village of Potter Heigham, four miles north of Clippesby Hall. Several boatyards hire out a variety of vessels by the hour or by the day, allowing tourists to enjoy the experience of piloting their own craft. For the less adventurous, Broads Tours (01692 670711) at Herbert Woods Boatyard offer piloted pleasure trips complete with running commentary.

When you first arrive at Clippesby Hall, don't be surprised if you're personally guided to your pitch; it's been a deliberate decision not to put large, obtrusive pitch-markers and unnecessary signs everywhere. After all, this is John's home and garden – it's been in the family for 50-odd years, and he doesn't want to ruin it by putting signs up everywhere to make it look like... well, like a campsite.

And that's the beauty of this unique place. It doesn't feel like a conventional commercial campsite. It has a far more agreeable atmosphere than that.

THE UPSIDE: Quiet and peaceful country site with good facilities.

THE DOWNSIDE: The swimming pool is too small to be much use, but is okay for a splash around.

THE DAMAGE: Prices for car, tent and 2 people from £10 in low season to £23 in high season.

THE FACILITIES: Swimming pool, grass tennis courts, kids' play area, crazy golf (£2), volleyball, football, Suzy's café and shop, family pub.

NEAREST DECENT PUB: The on-site pub is called The Muskett Arms and has a pub grub menu. About 6 miles away, The Fur and Feathers (01603 720003) in Woodbastwick, is a lovely country pub with a fantastic garden for the summer. It serves decent food and Woodforde ales (including the famous Norfolk Nog). The Woodforde Brewery (01603 722218) is next door and offers half-hour tours on certain evenings.

FOOD AND DRINK: The on-site shop sells local and fairtrade produce, and local ales and ciders can be had from the on-site pub.

IF IT RAINS: Tacky Great Yarmouth, Norfolk's busiest seaside resort, with amusement arcades, museums and a casino is only 10 miles away.

TREAT YOURSELF: To some one-to-one angling tuition and catch yourself a monster pike.

Professional angler Charlie Bettell (01603 714352) can arrange everything you need.

GETTING THERE: From the A47 between Norwich and Great Yarmouth, take the A1064 at Acle (Caister-on-Sea road). Take the first left at Clippesby onto the B1152 and follow the signs to Clippesby Hall.

PUBLIC TRANSPORT: The owners can pick you up from the station at Acle if you book in advance.

OPEN: Apr–Oct.

IF IT'S FULL: Just a couple of miles away is Woodside Farm (01692 670367), a tiny 10-pitch site in Thurne village with countryside views.

Clippesby Hall, Hall Lane, Clippesby, Norfolk NR29 3BL | t | 01493 367800 | w | www.clippesby.com

deer's glade

Contemporary bathrooms, wi-fi, an attentive concierge and a shuttle bus to the local pub. These may sound like hotel-style facilities, but it's all part of the service at Deer's Glade campsite.

Set in a quiet woodland clearing, Deer's Glade is a relatively new destination that successfully combines modern innovations with old-school camping principles. At first glance, it's not especially attractive. But on closer inspection, it's obvious that great care and attention has been taken in creating this site. The owners, David and Heather, apply great thought to everything they do. Sapling trees have been planted which, in time, will offer shade and shelter and will create a pleasant landscaped environment. The ground has been levelled and turfed for easy pitching. The slick shower facilities are housed in eco-friendly wooden buildings.

Here, customer comfort does not come at the expense of nature and conservation.

From the campsite, you can walk directly into the adjacent woodland, with acres of conifer-rich foliage and resident wild deer. The deer sometimes even visit the campsite, but it's easier to see them on the short walk to Gunton Park, which offers lovely parkland walks and a large, well-stocked fishing lake.

Two exceptional National Trust properties beg a visit. Felbrigg Hall is a remarkable 17th-century house, with a delightful walled garden and orangery. Near Aylsham, the fine Jacobean Blickling Hall is supposedly home to the headless ghost of Anne Boleyn.

These ancient houses hark back to an era of untold luxury. But for all their extravagance, even they never had wi-fi Internet access.

THE UPSIDE: Good fishing and easy walking from a peaceful campsite. Great seafood nearby.

THE DOWNSIDE: Trees are yet to mature, so the camping area is one big open space.

THE DAMAGE: Adults from £5–7.50 per night and children £1.75–2.75, depending on the season. There's a family deal of £13.50–18.50.

THE FACILITIES: Two spotless shower blocks with plenty of hot water; disabled and baby-changing facilities; on-site shop with tasty organic bacon and sausages; kids' play area; fishing available on site (£4.50) or next door at Gunton Hall (£4.50).

NEAREST DECENT PUB: The Alby Horse Shoes Inn (01263 761378) back on the main road is a traditional pub, with four real ales and a local-bias menu. If you're exploring the coast, the Red Lion Inn (01263 825408) in Upper Sheringham is worth stopping at, a 300-year-old pub with a Snug Bar and a menu featuring locally caught fish.

FOOD AND DRINK: Pick your own fruit and veg straight from the ground at Groveland Farm (01263 833777) in Roughton.

IF IT RAINS: Felbrigg Hall (01263 837444) and Blickling Hall (01263 738030) are within a few miles; Cromer and Sheringham on the coast are

well worth a visit; or check to see if Norwich FC (www.canaries.co.uk) are playing at home.

TREAT YOURSELF: To some Cromer crab at Cookies Crab Shop (01263 740352), Salthouse, where salads and platters come at bargain prices.

GETTING THERE: From Norwich, take the A140 towards Cromer. Five miles beyond Aylsham, turn right towards Suffield Green, signposted White Post Road. The site is half a mile on the right.

OPEN: All year.

IF IT'S FULL: The *Cool Camping* sites at Clippesby Hall (p132) and Pinewoods (p138) are both within easy reach.

Deer's Glade, White Post Road, Hanworth, Norwich, Norfolk NR11 7HN | t | 01263 768633 | w | www.deersglade.co.uk

pinewoods

Beach huts are a great British tradition. Maybe it's the fact that we can never trust the weather enough to be able to spend a whole day on the beach without shelter. Or maybe it's because most of us can't afford a home by the sea. Either way, these quirky little beach boxes have become an endearing symbol of the British seaside.

In recent years, beach huts have also become the sought-after alternative to a second home. In some parts of the country, these little wooden wonders have been known to change hands for more than £200,000. The alternative to purchasing your own beach hut is a trip to Pinewoods campsite at Wells-next-the-Sea on the north Norfolk coast, where you can rent one by the day or by the week, complete with deckchairs and a windbreak.

Pinewoods isn't a typical *Cool Camping* site. It's a big, commercial outfit with tenters often squeezed into a field by the boating lake. But in summer, they open up the Horse Paddock – a larger field where you can pick your own pitch and spread out sheltered by the tall grass. It's a trek from here to the amenities blocks, but portaloos and running water are to hand.

Holkham Hall, the local manor house, is still a family home to the Coke family, owners of much of this area, including Pinewoods campsite. You can't fail to be impressed by this immaculately maintained estate. But the one thing it lacks is a huge expanse of golden sand and direct sea view. You'll need a beach hut for that. Just as well the Coke family own those, too.

THE UPSIDE: Beach huts, sand dunes, miles of sandy beaches and the Norfolk Coast Path.

THE DOWNSIDE: Big, commercial site catering mainly for static holiday homes.

THE DAMAGE: Tents £9.25–£23.45 per night, depending on the season. Beach huts from £8.35 per day in low season to £23.75 midsummer.

THE FACILITIES: Several shower blocks with plenty of showers, toilets and washing-up sinks, kids' playground, well-stocked mini-market, coffee shop, boating lake with canoes and rowing boats for hire, trampolines, crazy golf, pool room.

NEAREST DECENT PUB: For a local pint and good-value bar food, The Globe Inn (01328 710206) in Wells is the best bet. The Victoria (01328 713230) is an exceptional gastropub at the entrance to Holkham Hall, with a changing restaurant menu featuring local ingredients.

FOOD AND DRINK: In Burnham Market, The Hoste Arms (01328 738777) continues to win accolades for its imaginative menu and well-priced wines.

IF IT RAINS: Historic Holkham Hall is 2 miles away, whilst the interesting seaside town of Cromer is not far in the other direction.

TREAT YOURSELF: To a night's stay with tip-top food at The Victoria or The Hoste Arms (see left).

GETTING THERE: Wells-next-the-Sea is 30 miles northwest of Norwich as the crow flies. From the A149 coast road, follow the signs to Wells and then to the beach. Pinewoods is almost at the end of Beach Road on the left.

PUBLIC TRANSPORT: Take the train to Kings Lynn and the popular Coast Hopper bus to Wells.

OPEN: Mar–Nov.

IF IT'S FULL: For a smaller campsite with a totally different vibe, check out High Sand Creek (01328 830119) at Stiffkey.

Pinewoods, Beach Road, Wells-next-the-Sea, Norfolk NR23 1DR	t	01328 710439	w	www.pinewoods.co.uk

deepdale farm

Come mid-September, most people of sound mind put tents, sleeping bags and any thoughts of camping to rest. It's not just because the days start to turn colder but because there aren't that many campsites that stay open once the leaves begin to curl and drop. Nudging the north Norfolk coastline, Deepdale Farm in Burnham Deepdale is a rare exception.

Alister and Jason Borthwick, the father-and-son team behind this beautiful expanse of arable land and campsite, insist that there is no better time to visit Norfolk than in autumn and winter. The hedgerows are pregnant with blackberries and poppies cheer from the country roadsides to make Norfolk a resplendent vision of russet-coloured forests and blush-coloured clouds. At dusk the sky is split by inky-black arrowheads of geese making their way en masse across the land to warmer climes, and behind the tents and tipis on Deepdale Farm, the hazy calm of miles of marshland is broken only by abandoned boats and impressive sails. As autumn creeps into winter, says Alister, it only gets better.

This philosophy goes some way to explaining the enthusiastic programme of events at the farm, with everything from organised stargazing and bird-watching through conservation walks and cycling to chilly winter dips and cookery classes with local produce. This farmer and his son's love of the locality, a designated Area Of Outstanding Natural Beauty, has not only encouraged an active social calendar but also created a campsite mindful of the environment; they encourage guests to do the same. In contrast to the landscape, camping here is not wild and woolly. With over 80 pitches accommodating tents and small camper vans, it's measured, considered and an air of responsible living pervades. The lights in the shower block operate on a motion sensor to avoid wasting electricity. Campers are respectfully asked to use the recycling bins, to throw on fir cones instead of synthetic firelighters and to heed the 10pm noise curfew.

If you hire one of the few tipis available, you will find it well maintained and orderly, equipped with a cast-iron chimenea for heat including paper, kindling and fuel for the fire, fold-away chairs, a BBQ and a lantern.

These are not tipis awash with Indian silks and ethnic blankets, but they don't need to be. Sleeping in the round with the wind whispering softly above you, through the top of your tipi, is enchantment enough. But even tipis, here furnished with mattresses covered in faux fur, can get chilly at night so make sure you pack a woolly hat and thick socks.

You might find yourself waking up at the darkest part of the night, just before dawn, with a cold nose; if you do, sneak a peek outside at the dazzlingly starry Norfolk sky. If you have been cooped up in a city for long enough, the sight will take your breath away.

There are plenty of diversions in and around Burnham Deepdale to keep you busy during the day. Kick-start the morning with a proper, frothy coffee at the café next door to the farm and stock up on necessities at the nearby supermarket or on-site camping shop before hiring a bike or stomping on your walking boots. If you find orienteering a bore then at

least make sure you take the short walk up to the forest at the other end of the farm, following the network of 'permissive bridleways'. You are so near to the coastline here, that a stroll down to the water's edge is also a must. It's particularly beautiful early in the morning when the tide is out.

Indian summer, late summer, the Season of Mellow Fruitfulness. Whatever you want to call this time of year when the pale sun is shining and the air is fresher than ever, it is a season to be savoured. A wholly different experience to lazy summer camping, this is vigorous, refreshing and invigorating.

THE UPSIDE: A winter wonderland. (Also open in the summer.)

THE DOWNSIDE: A strict 10pm noise curfew means drunken tomfoolery is not tolerated – a good thing if you need your sleep, a bad thing if the local ale (Old Les) and good company puts you in the mood for a party.

THE DAMAGE: Tent camping is charged per person per night: adults £4.50–8 and children £2.50–4, depending on the season. Tipis come in at a very reasonable £40–90 per night, depending on the time of year and the number of people.

THE FACILITIES: The site is equipped with eco-friendly hot showers, toilets and washing-up facilities. The water is heated by solar panels, with an oil burner back-up. Along with an on-site camping shop, the excellent Deepdale Café next

door serves everything from quality English breakfasts to chunky home-made soup.

NEAREST DECENT PUB: The White Horse (01485 210262) is about a 5-minute walk along the road. This buzzy, homely gastropub's dining room overlooks the dramatic marshland of Brancaster Staithe. Local fish and shellfish, when in season, include cockles, mussels and oysters from the 'beds' at the bottom of the garden.

FOOD AND DRINK: The Brancaster Brewery in the little fishing village of Brancaster Staithe produces a couple of fine ales, which you can buy at the Jolly Sailors (01485 210314) next door.

IF IT RAINS: Grab your mac and wellies and revel in it. Or escape to the posh boutiques of Burnham Market. It's not called Chelsea-on-Sea for nothing.

GETTING THERE: From the M11, take the A11, turning off to Swaffham. Then, head northwest on the A1065 towards Fakenham. Take the first exit at the roundabout onto Creake Road, then right onto the B1355, continuing to Burnham Market. Here there is a sharp left onto North Street before you need to turn right again, back onto the B1355 (Bellamy's Lane). A mile or so along the road, turn left onto the A149, and the farm is in front of you.

PUBLIC TRANSPORT: The nearest station is King's Lynn. From here, cycle or catch a CoastHopper bus 25 miles north east to Burnham Deepdale. Call 01553 776980 for bus times.

OPEN: All year.

IF IT'S FULL: Galley Hill Farm (01263 741201) in Blakeney is a peaceful, little campsite with easy access to the seal colony at Blakeney Point.

Deepdale Farm, Burnham Deepdale, Norfolk | t | 01485 210256 | w | www.deepdalefarm.co.uk

feather down farm

You're not, strictly speaking, 'camping' at a Feather Down Farm. You're staying in 'tented accommodation'. It's a small distinction, but it acts as a good indication of what you can expect at this mini-chain of boutique campsites. This is luxury camping in roomy three-bedroom pre-erected tents, perfect for the 'not sure about this camping lark' section of the community, who might baulk at the idea of trying to put up a tent in the rain. Or for families looking for a good-value alternative to renting a holiday home. Or, indeed, for just about anyone, really – these tented palaces are cool, comfortable and fun.

The Feather Down business model is little short of genius. They recruit farmers with excess, redundant land, then they transport and erect their high-spec, custom-designed tents at the farm, organise the marketing and reservations, and let the farmers take care of the day-to-day management. The Feather Down team and the farmers share the proceeds appropriately; and everyone's happy; the farmers benefit from low-investment diversification, and Feather Down have almost limitless access to expansion through the plentiful acreage of Britain's farming community.

But the other clever bit is the care and attention that has been lavished on the design of these tents to make camping here as comfortable and enjoyable as possible, even for longer stays. The tents are erected onto a raised wooden floor supported by a metal frame, which offers protection and insulation from the ground. The canvas covers reach to full height, to allow guests to walk around freely, and the living area is spacious, with a dining table and chairs, a cool box for food storage, a couple of deckchairs for comfy lounging and a wood-burning stove for heating and cooking. At the rear of the living area is the kitchen set-up, including a sink with running cold water (yes – running water! In a tent!) plus a work-top for food preparation and all crockery and cooking utensils. With two separate bedrooms, a further 'bunk room' for kids, and a flushing loo, this feels more like a cottage or holiday home, rather than a tent. There's no electricity, but candles and candelabra are provided for atmospheric, flame-lit evenings; and the cosy feel is enhanced by a colour scheme of autumnal tans and browns.

At Pettywood Farm (the Feather Down Farm location we stayed at between Peterborough and Grantham), some tents looked out onto the woodland and others were more exposed with views across the fields. But all were very much 'on the farm' with chickens whizzing and clucking around the place, and the excitable pigs screeching and snuffling in their adjacent pens. The sights, sounds, smells – and foods – of the farm are all part of the experience at Feather Down; fresh eggs can be gathered every morning from the henhouse, kids can learn about the animals and help feed them, and farm produce is available in the honesty-pantry. Big clumps of fat, juicy, wiggly carrots, caked in dirt and with foot-long sprouts are an absolute joy to handle and eat. A traditional wood-fired oven is also available for guests to use, and many of the farms organise a weekly communal pizza-firing evening during the summer.

The guys at Feather Down should be commended for their innovation. They've succeeded in designing truly superior tented accommodation and opening up the possibility of camping to those who might not have considered it before. It's also a good way of bringing people closer to the food they eat, gaining an understanding of what really goes on in the world of farming and reacquainting guests with the taste benefits of the freshest, local produce. No wonder it has been an instant hit, with the number of locations doubling in a year. Feather Down Farms are definitely on the up.

THE UPSIDE: Chic and comfortable farm camping in beautiful countryside surroundings.

THE DOWNSIDE: A farm-related soundtrack to your holiday.

THE DAMAGE: Weekend breaks £195–395 depending on season; a week in summer is £679.

THE FACILITIES: Double bed, two singles, one double 'bunk', flushing toilet, cool chest and wood-burning stove in each tent. Extra charge for linen and towels. There are clean portakabin-style showers and an organic 'honesty' farm pantry stocked with local produce, some tinned essentials, plus candles, matches and other useful items. Fresh eggs also available; watch your step, you could be stepping on breakfast!

NEAREST DECENT PUB: The Olive Branch (01780 410 355) at Clipsham won the Michelin 'Pub of the Year 2008' and is only a 5-minute drive (or a 20-minute walk) away and serves up delicious, locally sourced food. Advance bookings essential.

FOOD AND DRINK: Look no further than the farm on which you're staying for the freshest produce and cook it up yourself. Allow at least an hour for your stove to be hot enough to cook on.

IF IT RAINS: Light up the stove, crack open the playing cards and get cosy in your tent! Or visit Burghley House (01780 752451) in Stamford, a beautiful stately home.

TREAT YOURSELF: To traditional English cuisine with a contemporary flourish at The George

(01780 750750) in Stamford, about 10 minutes' drive from Pettywood Farm. Mains might cost up to £30, but this food is worth skipping lunch for!

GETTING THERE: Pettywood Farm is extremely difficult to find and involves finding a track marked by a tree and a telegraph pole! Full directions are supplied on reservation.

PUBLIC TRANSPORT: The nearest train stations are Stamford and Greenford. A pick-up can be arranged for a small fee.

OPEN: Mar–Oct.

IF IT'S FULL: There are 12 other Feather Down Farm campsites across the UK, all situated on working farms and offering a similar experience.

Feather Down Farm, Pettywood Farm, Holywell, Stamford, Lincolnshire		
t	01420 80804	w	www.featherdown.co.uk

bracelands

The Forestry Commission certainly know how to run a good campsite; they own over 20 campsites across Britain and some of the finest forest land in the country. So, you're guaranteed a site surrounded by woodland, with well-marked forest walks and cycle routes, scenic forest drives, picnic sites and play areas. It's also a good bet you'll have some of Britain's best-kept countryside on your doorstep.

Bracelands campsite in the Forest of Dean is no exception. The huge camping meadow on the upper slopes of the Wye Valley is surrounded by dense forest on all sides. Even the camping fields are dotted with the occasional copper beech tree.

The facilities are faultless. Rows and rows of pristine toilets and showers are arranged in three shower blocks. Of course, there's a genuine need for all these facilities with 520 pitches and up to 2000 visitors to cater for.

An easy walk through the forest delivers you at the banks of the Wye River, which is passable via the suspension bridge at Bilblins, or stay on this side for a delightful walk to Symonds Yat.

On the Forest Of Dean Sculpture Trail you'll discover trees interspersed with sculptures and works of art; a thoroughly enjoyable 3½-mile stroll through the landlord's extensive acreage.

THE UPSIDE: Well-managed campsite in the heart of the Forest of Dean.
THE DOWNSIDE: Colossal site with 520 pitches.
THE DAMAGE: Reception is next door at the Christchurch site. Prices per pitch per night including 2 adults start at £10.60 during the week and £11.70 at weekends.
THE FACILITIES: Hot and cold water, showers, baby-changing facilities, laundry, chemical disposal point, electric hook-ups, payphone, disabled facilities, dogs welcome. There's a shop next to reception at the Christchurch site.

NEAREST DECENT PUB: The King of Spain (01594 834859) is an okay pub within walking distance, with wholesome grub and Greene King IPA. But it's well worth visiting the excellent Saracens Head Inn at nearby Symonds Yat.
FOOD AND DRINK: Three Choirs Vineyard (01531 890223) in Newent is England's leading single-estate vineyard. And they have a restaurant, too, so you can make a day of it.
IF IT RAINS: Bristol is an easy drive from here; as is the literary town of Hay-on-Wye.
TREAT YOURSELF: To some off-roading 4x4 style at Whitecliff Off Road Driving (01594 834666).

GETTING THERE: From the A40, take the A4136 towards Coleford. Stay on this road until it crosses the B4432 at the Pike House Inn. Take the B4432 towards Symonds Yat then turn left, following the campsite signs. Bracelands reception is at Christchurch campsite, next door.
PUBLIC TRANSPORT: Take the train to Lydney and then bus it to the Christchurch crossroads, from where it's just a 3–4-minute walk to the site.
OPEN: Mar–Nov.
IF IT'S FULL: Christchurch campsite (0845 130 8224) next door is a smaller, sheltered and dog-free site but with even better facilities.

Bracelands, Bracelands Drive, Christchurch, Coleford, Gloucestershire GL16 7NN

| t | 0845 130 8224 | w | www.forestholidays.co.uk |

woodland tipis

If you go down to the woods today, you're in for a big surprise. Not a teddy bear's picnic, but a small gathering of Sioux Indian tipis and yurts – along with a large clay pizza oven! This unique setting lies hidden in the heart of a magical woodland, nestled neatly between Ross-on-Wye and Hereford.

Julia Sanders created this wonderland on an unused part of her parents' farm, after her application for eco-lodges was turned down by the local council. And the setting couldn't be more perfect; an enchanting little 11-acre forest and private grassland valley with views across the Malvern Hills.

The two yurts and three tipis are scattered around an ancient woodland that has been undisturbed for years, bar the mystical creatures and fairies that are said to inhabit the bluebells at the bases of the trees. Ready-made tracks – originally built for the previous owner's huskies' sledging practice – loop the forest floor. They're perfect for racing through the woods and collecting bow-and-arrow sticks and makeshift fishing rods with which to catch dinner, in the pond at the bottom of the valley.

Each tent is cosily laid out with sheepskin rugs, raised mattresses and plenty of additional blankets for those extra chilly nights. Most importantly, there's also a wood-burning stove and a kettle in each one for that first cuppa in the morning. Outside there's a campfire, log-style tables and chairs and your own personal hammock. The tipis are all slightly different and each seems to have its own distinct personality. For the best view, go for Valley tipi, the name alluding to the panorama that awaits. Yonder yurt is the most secluded option – great for a romantic weekend.

The facilities are first-rate and thoughtfully put together. First, and most importantly, the showers are better than home. The fully stocked kitchen has everything you could possibly want and a separate fridge is assigned to each tipi. There are fresh flowers in an eclectic collection of vases scattered charmingly all over the site; lanterns and candles add to the already tranquil ambience. Swinging ropes and ladders make this a kids' paradise whilst the grown-ups have their own covered communal area with furniture made from old school desks and benches. A real back-to-childhood feel, in a good way.

On arrival there's a welcome note chalked onto a board with the name of your tent and a handy wheelbarrow to lug your stuff down to the car-free campsite. Then follows a quick lesson on how to make a fire in the middle of the tipi, without asphyxiating everyone. Now, who wants to head for the hills?

With easy access to the Forest of Dean and the Malvern Hills, walkers are spoilt for choice. But there's also kayaking on the many meandering Wye Valley waterways or swinging from high wires in tree-top canopies at Go Ape. The quaint market towns of Ross-on-Wye and the more literary Hay-on-Wye are also worth exploring before heading back to begin the task of fire making and pizza burning.

As the kids run around playing cowboys and Indians in the woods, this magical place may well bring out your inner child. It's a real woodland adventure, scented by the heady aroma of campfires – and scrummy home-made pizzas slowly cooking in the communal oven.

THE UPSIDE: Tipi-camping and pizza-making in a magical woodland setting.

THE DOWNSIDE: It's difficult to find a downside.

THE DAMAGE: All tipis and yurts sleep 4–5 people. Weekend rates (3 nights) are £220 for yurts and £195 for tipis. In high season, weekly prices go up to £495 for yurts and £450 for tipis.

THE FACILITIES: There are 2 yurts and 3 tipis, each with 2 or 3 double mattresses, blankets, kettle and wood-burning stove. There are 3 great showers, flush toilets and 1 composting toilet, a well-stocked covered kitchen with seating and the famous pizza and bread oven! Outside there is a covered communal area, hammocks and a shop selling home-made soup and basic supplies.

NEAREST DECENT PUB: You're spoilt for choice. The epitome of gastropub cuisine (and a choice of 80 beers!) can be found at the New Harp Inn in nearby Hoarwithy (01432 840900). The Lough Pool Inn in Sellack (01989 730236) has a beer garden, and the invitingly named Cottage of Content sits on a 4-mile stretch of the River Wye just below Little Dewchurch (01432 840 242). All sell local ales and tasty, mostly organic food (main courses around £10-12).

FOOD AND DRINK: Pengethley Farm Shop in Peterstow (01989 730430) stocks organic sausages, cheese and olives.

IF IT RAINS: A tour around Weston's Cider Farm (01531 660233) in Much Marcle, 8 miles away, is a tasty day out.

TREAT YOURSELF: To a high-wired forest adventure with 'Go Ape!' at Mallards Pike Lake (0870 4589078).

GETTING THERE: From A49 to Hereford, turn right to Hoarwithy and Little Dewchurch. Carry on 5 miles through Hoarwithy village, up steep hill for 1 mile. Woodlands Farm is on the left.

PUBLIC TRANSPORT: Catch the train to Hereford; bus 37 (from Hereford or Ross-on-Wye) passes by the farm every two hours (Young's Coaches; 01531 821584).

OPEN: Easter–Sep.

IF IT'S FULL: Head to Tresseck Campsite (01432 840235) in Hoarwithy for a peaceful riverside location, to launch a kayak or do a spot of fishing.

Woodland Tipis and Yurt Holidays, Woodlands Farm, Little Dewchurch, Herefordshire HR2 6QD

| | t | 01432 840488 | w | www.woodlandtipis.co.uk |

eastnor castle

In days gone by, more embarrassing than having your underpants caught in your breeches, was your mansion ceiling found to be lacking in the height department. It was a sign of impending financial collapse and a notice that you were a hair's breadth away from state benefits. So, to keep up with the Jones's, the first Earl of Somers buried the original mansion at Eastnor under a lake and threw up a vast Gothic Georgian castle in its place; this time with a lofty 17.5-metre (58-ft) ceiling in the main hallway.

The current owner and occupier of this magnificent family home, James Hervey-Bathurst, has thoughtfully preserved every inch of ceiling height and period features; although, he added that all-important modern necessity – central heating. Within the castle, each of the nine double bedrooms has its own character and attendant luxuries; most notably the plush four-poster-bedded Red room. And tempting as it would be to stay here, you will need a healthy bank balance and 10 good friends to gain exclusive pillow rights.

An arboretum, a lake, and a road away from the impressive castle lies the deer park where you'll be pitching your tent for the night. A designated Area of Outstanding Natural Beauty and Special Scientific Interest, it's a sweeping vista of rolling hills and hidden pockets of woodland nooks and crannies.

The whole vibe about the place is pretty chilled. You just pitch up, literally, and settle in. The park warden will wander by to collect your money and he serves as a security measure, too, as the park is open to the public during the day and several footpaths criss-cross the park.

When choosing a pitch it's definitely worth taking a drive around the whole park before deciding on that perfect spot. There are plenty of flat sites along the two coarse-fishing lakes and valley floor, but for a tent with a view go higher up the hill under an ancient oak and the backdrop of the stately castle. Come evening time, the sun may even play ball and drop conveniently behind the castle walls in a picture-postcard kind of way.

The park's vast tracts of land open onto the majestic Malvern Hills. You can roll off your ground mat and be heading hillward in the time it takes you to kneel down and tie your bootlaces or clip on your cycle shoes. You can either follow the well-marked paths or head into the Ledbury tourist office (two miles away) and pick up one of the staggering number of alternative routes and maps available there.

This really laid-back place does come with a price: a lack of the usual campsite facilities. There are water points and cesspits but no showers or toilets. The absence of toilet and shower blocks explains why there are more caravanners than campers here. So, why not even out the numbers and bring your own portable chemical toilet and, if you can cope with an out-in-the-open type of cleansing, a solar shower, too?

The ample space and chilled *chakras* are presumably why The Big Chill chose this peaceful 600-acre spot for their annual festival. The park closes for this and other big events so it's worth calling ahead to check what's on; or thousands of mad mountain-bikers may descend on the park and get in the way of your perfectly pitched tent.

After a day out pounding the hills, it's all about sitting back, drink in hand, enjoying the vista and spaciousness of the castle grounds. And as you take in the view, sneak a peek at the height of your fellow campers' canvas ceilings; you may want to upgrade your tent next time you visit the camping shop.

THE UPSIDE: Mountains of open space in the grounds of a fairy tale castle.

THE DOWNSIDE: No facilities; which means most other guests are in caravans.

THE DAMAGE: Family tents and caravans cost £6.50 per night; single tents are £3 per person per night. Campers get half-price castle admission when it's open.

THE FACILITIES: There are no toilets, showers, electric hook-ups or waste collection. There are ample water points and cesspits. Free coarse-fishing in two lakes. No campfires but raised BBQs are allowed; collect wood from the forest.

NEAREST DECENT PUB: The Quills restaurant in The Feathers Hotel (High Street, Ledbury; 01531 635266) has bags of atmosphere and platefuls of delicious food that changes every evening.

FOOD AND DRINK: Also on Ledbury's High Street is Ceci Paulo – a cooking emporium on three floors with an exquisite Italian deli, restaurant, fashions and cooking lessons (01531 632976).

IF IT RAINS: Wander through Eastnor Castle with its Knight's Maze, kids' assault course and adventure playground. In the bothy in the castle grounds you can try out one of many Land Rover adventure courses (to book call 0844 848 4469).

TREAT YOURSELF: To a ticket to The Big Chill festival (see p253).

GETTING THERE: Leave M50 at junction 2, following A417 into Ledbury. Turn right onto A449 (signed Worcester and Malvern). One mile on, turn right onto A438 Eastnor. Past the castle, the sign for Eastnor deer park is 500 metres on the left.

PUBLIC TRANSPORT: There are direct trains from London Paddington to Ledbury, 2 miles away. Buses (0870 6082608; www.herefordbus.info) connect through Ledbury from Hereford, Ross and Great Malvern. Buses 388, 244 and 476 will get you to Eastnor on the Hereford to Cheltenham service once a day.

OPEN: Easter–Sep.

IF IT'S FULL: It's never full, but it's a good idea to check what events are running in the park as this may affect your camping experience.

Eastnor Castle, Ledbury, Herefordshire, HR8 1RL | t | 01531 633160 | w | www.eastnorcastle.com

middle woodbatch farm

You might find it hard to place Shropshire on a map of the UK. Not many people live in West Midland's little-known county on the border of England and Wales – Shropshire boasts one of the lowest populations per square mile in England – and the rest of us, the tourists, are largely unaware of its colourful past.

Rich in archaeological and geological splendours, most of the sloping landscape was formed during the Ice Age. More than 20 hill forts tell of the county's battles during the Iron Age (600BC); then there are over 30 castles dotted alongside numerous abbeys, lakes and canals, which, if walls could talk, would regale us with many a tale of feuding battles.

Bishops Castle is a small medieval market town in the Shropshire Hills. A local population of artists, musicians and craftsmen adds a slight bohemian edge to the tiny high street. Several arty shops offer attentive service and will encourage your custom, before waving you off to one of the local pubs to toast your purchases with a pint of own-brewed ale.

As you pootle down the mile-long lane that leads out of the town towards Middle

Woodbatch Farm, you'll find the countryside comfort of being sandwiched by leafy hedgerows extremely calming. Steven Austin grew up on this working farm, which has been in his family since 1936. Along with his partner Mary, he now raises cows, sheep and hens. In 2006 the couple opened their first camping field, where they greet arrivals with the warmest of welcomes, with the help of two Sams – their young son and the dog.

The Austins operate a policy of admitting only 10 tents or camper vans at a time. You could even get the field to yourself in low season, where you'll see the Shropshire Hills roll out before you like a sea of green grass, as sheep graze like buoys bobbing in the breeze. The campsite boasts many other bonus points. Children will like the farm animals, which also include a pet pig and a magnificent dapple-grey mare called Molly. Then, there's all the sheep, which Steven might well need help herding.

The family is busy all year round. Lambing on the farm – a hit with young and old – takes places in April. Whilst in June, a burgeoning international walking festival attracts regular and repeat custom, so book well ahead. Other local activities include a Michaelmas Fair, Real Ale and Food Festival and a Tandem Triathlon; there always seems to be something going on.

Whenever you fancy a spot of exploring then the ruined castle at nearby Clun is well worth a visit. As is The Stiperstones where you'll find the 'Devil's Chair' ridge amongst the rocky outcrops, a locale for one of D. H. Lawrence's scenes in his novel *St Mawr*. There are myriad walks in the area, but we reckon the best one is the 15-mile Kerry Ridgeway route to Powys (an ancient route to Montgomery overlooking Churchstoke and the Camlad valley), with its 70-mile long views in good weather.

If you're not a keen campfire cook, or fancy a treat after a long day's hike, you can pre-book a two-course dinner sourced from regionally produced or organic products, either to eat in the farmhouse kitchen or to take back to your tent. Mary also knocks up full English breakfasts for a fiver. If you're on a budget, though, just buy some farm eggs and rustle up something yourself in the campers' own purpose-built kitchenette.

For an ultimate escape within easy reach of cities such as Manchester and Birmingham, South Shropshire is low in human traffic and high in spiritually enriching nature. It's an enviable paradise for locals and an ideal camping climate for the rest of us.

THE UPSIDE: A lovely, small site, far from city life, and with hearty home cooking on tap.

THE DOWNSIDE: The animals wake early; pack earplugs.

THE DAMAGE: Adults are £5 per night and it's £2 for children over 10, under-10s go free.

THE FACILITIES: Two large shower rooms (£1 donations requested) are newly built and comfortable with non-slip, cushioned flooring – proper camping luxury! A basic kitchenette is equipped with a microwave, fridge and kettle.

NEAREST DECENT PUB: At the end of the winding road is the Six Bells (01588 630144), a former coaching inn dating back to 1670, which serves own-brewed ales. Take a torch if you're

walking, or the hosts may give you a lift. It doesn't serve food on Sunday or Monday evenings.

FOOD AND DRINK: Willo Game (01588 650539) are wild game wholesale dealers based at Bishop's Gate, the heart of pheasant countryside. They sell seasonal produce such as venison, partridge, rabbits and award-winning boar and apricot sausages all over the UK, including three of the village's pubs (Castle Gate, The Boars Head and the Three Tuns Inn).

IT IF RAINS: The House on Crutches Museum (01588 630007) will kill 10 minutes. A 16th-century timber-framed building raised above ground level on 'crutches' it has a small, history exhibition. The Bishops Castle Railway and

Transport Museum (01588 638446) takes a look at the once-famous local railway.

GETTING THERE: It's off the A488, accessed from the A49/A489, 22 miles south of Shrewsbury, 18 miles north east of Ludlow. Head to the bottom of town along Station Street, turning right at the Six Bells and then first left. The farm is signposted from there.

PUBLIC TRANSPORT: The Secret Hills shuttle bus runs from April to October (01588 673888).

OPEN: Mar–Oct.

IF IT'S FULL: Nearby Foxholes Castle Camping (01588 638924) is set in 28 acres, so it is a much larger site. Set in beautiful countryside it has modern facilities and is big on recycling.

Middle Woodbatch Farm, Woodbatch Road, Bishops Castle, Shropshire SY9 5JS

| | t | 01588 630141 | w | www.middlewoodbatchfarm.co.uk |

small batch

For the past 500 million years, the area now known as Shropshire has had it tough. It's been pushed south towards the Antarctic, spat out the earth's crust and then pulled back north to where it sits today. It has sunk under the sea, reinvented itself as a coral reef, spent time near the sub-tropical equator and finally settled in its most recent location, along a fairly quiet fault line. The upshot of all this geographical to-ing and fro-ing is a fantastically varied landscape; and you'll experience this first hand at Small Batch campsite.

And this hotbed of geological activity is indicative of the huge number of activities there are to get out amongst this landscape. Hang-gliding from Longmynd peak gives you a chance to see it all from a unique vantage point, as does paragliding, cycling the miles of quiet country lanes and even playing a round of golf. The Church Stretton golf course is one of the highest courses in England, so you can blame any hooked shots on the distraction of the breathtaking views. And then there's the Longmynd hike. Every year at the beginning of October, a smallish group of extreme hikers takes to the Shropshire hills to attempt a crazy, boot-wearying 50-mile hike. The challenge is to leg it up (and down) eight of the region's summits in under 24 hours. Why, you might reasonably ask? Possibly, because it seemed like a good idea over a pint or two.

If this level of energy-sapping activity is not what you signed up for, there are plenty of far more sedate walks in this designated Area of Outstanding Natural Beauty. One of these conveniently starts from the charming Small Batch campsite nestled at the base of Longmynd. It's a less arduous seven-mile round trip that conveniently deposits you in the local Green Dragon pub a mere four hours later and within spitting distance of your tent.

This tranquil riverside site is perfect for walkers and twitchers alike, and there are many chances to see a buzzard or red kite soaring in the rarified air above. It's also a handy base for a gentle meandering through the vibrant market towns of Ludlow, Shrewsbury or historic Bishops Castle. It is a small, secluded site, which has its advantages but it can mean you're a bit close to your neighbours when it's full. There also seem to be an awful lot of rules, which can feel a bit unnecessary and overbearing. The upside is that it's been in the current Prince family for 39 years, enough time to gather a wealth of knowledge about the various routes up the Longmynd and other ridges. If the friendly owners can't help you then try the town's Information Centre, two miles down the road. They have a supply of maps that will inspire you to pull on the socks, tighten those bootlaces and start walking.

If the merest mention of hiking leaves you quaking in your boots, then the various routes of the Shropshire Hills Shuttle could be your answer. It takes you up hill and down dale via some jaw-dropping views,

and requires no more energy than pushing the shutter button on your camera. And if eating and drinking the local grub sounds more your sort of thing then come in July for the town's annual cake and ale trail.

Whether you like your holiday fast-paced and activity laden or charmingly chilled out, it's up to you how much moving around you do. There is enough activity here to warrant another shift in the earth's crust – but it's unlikely to happen again for another million years or so.

THE UPSIDE: Fall out your tent and start walking.
THE DOWNSIDE: The rules.
THE DAMAGE: £10 per tent per night, £12 per caravan and £2 electric hook-up.
THE FACILITIES: The 24 pitches are served by basic but good showers, toilets and washing-up area. Electric hook-ups, waste unit at main house. Dogs allowed.
NEAREST DECENT PUB: Two pubs within stumbling distance from the campsite are worth a try: The Green Dragon (01694 722925) and the slightly more atmospheric Ragleth Inn (01694 722711). Both serve real ales and decent, wholesome food.

FOOD AND DRINK: There's plenty of yummy farmer's markets stocking local organic goodies; Church Stretton (2nd/4th Fri), Ludlow (2nd Thurs), Craven Arms (1st Sat) and Bishops Castle (3rd Sat).
IF IT RAINS: For all things ancient, follow the antiques trail at Stretton Antiques Market, Church Stretton (01694 723718).
TREAT YOURSELF: To a high-altitude adventure, hang-gliding off Longmynd peak. Beyond Extreme (01691 682640), based in Church Stretton, can organise any number of other thrills and spills.
GETTING THERE: From the A49, follow signs to Shrewsbury/Church Stretton. Then take the B5477 signed Little Stretton. Turn left beside The Ragleth Inn, opposite the hard-to-miss thatched church.

Take the next right, then continue straight ahead through the ford to find the campsite.
PUBLIC TRANSPORT: Church Stretton (2 miles away) has a train station where hourly services run between Cardiff and Manchester (Arriva; 0845 6061660). Connect at Newport from London. Bus 435 (TESS; 01588 673888) goes via The Ragleth Inn every 2 hours. The handy Shropshire Hills Shuttle (www.shropshirehillsshuttles.co.uk) will also take you all or part of the way up every single peak on the weekends/Bank Holidays.
OPEN: Easter–Sep.
IF IT'S FULL: Try The Coates Farm (01694 771330), 5 miles away just the other side of Church Stretton, for a similar quiet rural vibe.

Small Batch Campsite, Little Stretton, Church Stretton, Shropshire SY6 6PW

| | t | 01694 723358 | w | www.smallbatch-camping.webeden.co.uk |

longnor wood

In the southern 'White Peak' area of the Peak District, surrounded by shallow hills, sits the village of Longnor. It's an idyllic place with a cobbled market square, pretty cottages fashioned from local stone and a thriving industry in clockmaking. The slow-paced, old-world ambience is enhanced by the gentle melody of peeling church bells. An inscription above the old market hall lists the tariffs for trading here – as of 1873.

It's the sort of place that city dwellers visit for a weekend and immediately decide they'd like to move to. Most don't, of course, but Paul and Lindsey Hedges did. Already keen campers and on the lookout for a lifestyle change from their careers in bricklaying and banking, they came across Longnor Wood – a campsite on the outskirts of the village. Its current owners were moving on and it was up for sale. Within a few short months, they'd snapped it up, ditched their jobs and moved their lives from urban Bristol to rural Derbyshire.

They then set about creating the sort of campsite they would want to stay in. It was already an adults-only site when they took it over and the absence of kids running around seemed fitting for such a peaceful location amongst the dales. So, the rule remained. They set aside some of the 20 acres for wildlife, planted more trees to screen the tents from the surrounding hills and opted for as spacious pitches as they could accommodate.

The result is a tranquil campsite that maximises the great location and minimises its environmental impact. Three small, gently sloping fields are surrounded by woods and farmland, offering tantalising glimpses of the Peak National Park.

All the essential facilities are here, but Paul and Lindsey have made a conscious decision not to pander to the extravagant needs of satellite-TV campers. They've avoided cash-generating super-pitches and electricity in the camping fields, not just for environmental reasons but because it goes against the spirit of camping. With stunning countryside all around, why would anyone want to sit inside and watch TV?

Extra touches include a French-style *boules* court, a nine-hole putting green and badminton court. But Paul and Lindsey are keen to stress that the campsite's major attractions are not on the site at all, but all

The market town of Buxton, home to a natural warm-water spring discovered by the Romans, is only six miles away. It's sometimes known as the Bath of the north – given the similarity to its better-visited southern cousin – and not just for its spa credentials. Grand Georgian and Victorian architecture dominates its historic core, where a sweeping curve of houses is reminiscent of the famous Bath Royal Crescent. The lovingly restored Opera House here is well worth a visit; tours are available on Saturday mornings at 11am, or if you're visiting during the July Opera Festival, you might be lucky enough to get a ticket for a performance. On Tuesdays and Saturdays Market Place comes alive with a plethora of stalls, friendly, vocal stallholders and browsing shoppers. This spot is also the centre for eating and drinking in Buxton, with numerous little cafés and restaurants.

Longnor Wood is an ideal base for walking amongst the rugged scenery of the Peak District. Easily followed paths criss-cross the nearby Upper Dove and Manifold Valleys with a variety of routes for all abilities. The distinguished walks and views around here are quite something, with Dove Ridge, in particular, the place to head to for a stunning outlook and gentle inspiration. Who knows, you might even end up wanting to move here.

THE UPSIDE: Well-run campsite with dale views – and no kids! (That'll be an upside for some and a downside for others.)

THE DOWNSIDE: Can get busy in summer and on Bank Holidays. No kids.

THE DAMAGE: A tent and up to 2 people is £15 per night, standard caravan/motorhome pitch £17 and an extra person £5.

THE FACILITIES: Heated toilet block, hot showers, shop, laundry room, *boules*, badminton and putting. The on-site shop sells eggs from the local farm.

NEAREST DECENT PUB: There are a few decent pubs in Longnor, but a mile further on is the outstanding Packhorse Inn (01298 83618) in Crowdecote, a beautiful old limestone pub with a reputation for good food and tasty ales. It'll take just over half an hour to walk there, quite possibly longer to walk back.

FOOD AND DRINK: Chatsworth's farm shop (01246 565300) has a huge range of local produce with local butchers and bakers on site. And they have tastings and cookery demos.

IF IT RAINS: Buxton has everything you need to make a rainy weekend fun. Tour the Opera House (0845 1272190) or enjoy cream teas Edwardian-style at Hargreaves Coffee Shop (01298 23083).

TREAT YOURSELF: To some post-canvas pampering at Blenheim House (01283 732254).

GETTING THERE: Longnor is 6 miles southeast of Buxton. From Longnor, follow the brown caravan signs along the Longnor-Leek road for 1 mile.

PUBLIC TRANSPORT: Catch the train to Buxton then bus it to Longnor, from where you'll have to walk the mile to the site.

OPEN: Mar–Oct.

IF IT'S FULL: Just off the A6 at Blackwell-in-the-Peak is Cottage Farm Caravan Park (01298 85330), a compact site with Peak views.

Longnor Wood Caravan and Camping Park, Longnor, nr Buxton, Derbyshire SK17 0NG

| | t | 01298 83648 | w | www.longnorwood.co.uk |

north lees

Shielded within a grove of oak- and beech-lined woodland, lies the North Lees National Trust campsite. An idyllic-sounding setting in its own right, but add to that the looming slopes of England's largest cliff above the distant treeline and the site's babbling brook of a beck and what you get is just about as near a state of natural perfection as you're likely to find.

The site itself is fairly basic. There's no play area for the kids, but they'll find natural entertainment enough frolicking within the plentiful woodlands, and the stream provides a handy damming project.

Set across four fields, North Lees feels deceptively smaller than its actual size, with the trees and dry-stone walls acting to shield each field from the other. The whole site sits on a gentle slope as the ground around begins its ascent up to the moor's peak at Stanage Edge.

At North Lees you're deep in the heart of the setting for Jane Austen's novel *Pride and Prejudice*. So, whilst you're here, why not recreate the iconic shot from the 2005 film version in which Keira Knightley's fast-witted Elizabeth Bennett stands atop The Edge, looking out over the swathes of Derbyshire? You can walk up the slopes to Stanage Edge easily from a track at the back of the site. 'The Edge' stretches for six miles with its cliff of gritstone reaching a height of 25 metres in some places. The tall face of the cliff is a Mecca for climbers, ascending the boulder-strewn ridge-line that juts out of the ground. Most days of the week you'll be able to crane your neck upwards to watch climbers ascend the face and you'll probably find yourself holding your breath whilst you do so. The site's proximity to Stanage means it's a regular hang-out for the climbing conscious, but, no fear, there's no 'us and them' atmosphere. Everyone's content just to kick back and soak up some of Mother Nature's ambience.

Ascending The Edge needn't be done at the end of a rope, though. You can wander on up and find your own route to take in the expansive views. From up here you'll wonder at the patchwork quilt of colours, from verdant green to the scorched brown fields, managed for the red grouse. A walk up to the cliff's face means navigating the randomly strewn boulders – it's like wandering around the building site of the Gods.

Nearby Chatsworth House is in on the Jane Austen act, too, having starred as Mr Darcy's Pemberley pile in the 2005 film. But it offers heaps more than film-star credentials. A wander around the house itself unveils walls dripping with priceless paintings, neo-classical statues and works from Old Masters. Outside, the gardens, if you can call them that, are the product of five centuries of green-thumbed craftsmanship, with a willow tree that's really a fountain, classical water spouting statues and the infamous cascading waterfalls. All of which, unsurprisingly, draws over 300,000 visitors a year and keeps 120 gardeners busy.

The Peak District draws in 45 million day-visitors a year and given the landscape and its historical houses it's no surprise. But at North Lees you could feel like you're amongst the only few people in the park, protected behind the walls of this secluded woodland.

THE UPSIDE: A lovely woodland setting alive with the sounds of the forest.

THE DOWNSIDE: A small number of pitches means that it's often booked up.

THE DAMAGE: Adults £4.50 per night, £3 for children (6–14s) and students £3.50; under 5s go free. Cars £1–2 per night. Prices go up by 50p over Bank Holidays but you'll get a 50p/per night discount if you arrive on public transport.

THE FACILITIES: There are on-site recycling facilities, hot showers, with male and female toilet blocks, a washing-up area and a drying room.

NEAREST DECENT PUB: The tucked-away Little John Inn (01433 650 225) down the road in Hathersage offers local micro-brew ales and decent pub fare in its wood-panelled interior.

FOOD AND DRINK: The Scotsmans Pack (01433 650 253) has a new selection of micro-brew ales every month, with local fish and meat on its menu.

IF IT RAINS: Get more of an Austen fix at nearby Chatsworth House (01246 565300).

TREAT YOURSELF: To some gliding lessons or a trial glide with the Derbyshire and Lancashire Gliding Club (01298 871270) at Camphill.

GETTING THERE: Take the A6187 eastbound toward Hathersage. After about 2 miles, turn left up Jagger Lane and then left up Coggers Lane. Watch out for the Birley Lane turn-off about 2 miles on your right. The site is about 1 mile on the left.

PUBLIC TRANSPORT: Get the train to Stanage and it's approximately a mile's walk up to the campsite. Call in advance for detailed directions.

OPEN: Easter–Dec.

IF IT'S FULL: Hardhurst Farm campsite (01433 620001) offers chilled out countryside camping in the heart of the Hope Valley.

North Lees National Trust Campsite, Birley Lane, Hathersage, Derbyshire S33 1BR | t | 01433 650 838

fieldhead

Question: What's the busiest National Park in Europe and the second busiest in the world after Mount Fuji? Unexpected answer: The Peak District in England's Midlands.

The Peak District is a unique and striking wilderness with a rare diversity of landscapes – from peaty bogs and tall cliffs to green fields and rolling hills. And in the middle of it all, you'll find Fieldhead campsite in Edale, a rambler's paradise with some of the best walking in England.

The site is a popular launch pad for the Pennine Way, an epic 270-mile path that starts in Edale and heads north along the Pennine Ridge, through the Yorkshire Dales and Northumberland, finishing up at the Scottish Borders. You might not want to attempt the whole path, but the first leg, from Edale to Cowden is a good taster.

The campsite is made up of five intimately sized fields set at varying levels on a riverside hillock with plenty of shelter provided by fences and hedges. There are no marked pitches, so just pick an area that suits you. It's a small campsite, so nowhere is really far from the amenities block.

The quiet, countryside feel of Fieldhead is enhanced by the fact that cars cannot be driven onto the site. Simply deposit your vehicle in the car park at the entrance (don't forget to reserve a space when booking your pitch) and transfer your gear to your tent.

Whether you're following the path well trod across the Pennines or discovering the lesser-trampled treasures of Edale, Fieldhead – a perfect base camp – will get you off on the right foot.

THE UPSIDE: Fantastic walking from this miniature campsite.

THE DOWNSIDE: The trains can be noisy during the night and the insects a bit friendly at dusk.

THE DAMAGE: Tents only. Adults from £3.50 to £5 per person per night, children £2.50–3.50. Parking is £1.50–3.

THE FACILITIES: Hot showers are 20p, so bring some coins! Disabled facilities, washing-up area and laundry services available. No shop on site – there's a general stores in town, but don't rely on it, bring everything you need. Dogs allowed.

NEAREST DECENT PUB: The Ramblers Inn (01433 670268) in Edale is a well-presented renovation of an old pub, serving real ales and reasonable food. You can survey the scenery from the beer garden. Folk music nights on occasional Wednesdays through the summer can be great fun.

FOOD AND DRINK: Eighteen miles away, Fischer's Baslow Hall (01246 583259) has a Michelin-starred restaurant. The menu is mouth watering.

IF IT RAINS: The local settlement of Castleton is home to several dramatic caves, including Peak Cavern (01433 620512) and Speedwell Cavern (01433 620512), both of which have guided tours.

TREAT YOURSELF: To a night at the dogs at Owlderton Stadium (0114 2343074) in Sheffield.

GETTING THERE: Edale is about 10 miles northeast of Buxton. Follow the signs for Edale from the A265. As you approach the village, Fieldhead is on the right just after The Ramblers Inn.

PUBLIC TRANSPORT: Take the Hope Valley line to Edale and walk to the site from the station.

OPEN: All year.

IF IT'S FULL: Coopers Campsite (01433 670372) is a larger site on the same road that takes caravans and motorhomes as well as tents.

Fieldhead Campsite, Edale, Hope Valley, Derbyshire S33 7ZA | t | 01433 670386 | w | www.fieldhead-campsite.co.uk

upper booth farm

What can you do when crowds of people – all total strangers – insist on walking through your garden? Thousands of them, in fact. Tramping around with big muddy boots and walking sticks, chattering away excitedly; the inconsiderate wretches.

Of course, this isn't your bog-standard garden. This is 970 acres of prime Derbyshire livestock farmland in one of the most renowned valleys in the Peak District. It's also the home and garden of Robert and Sarah Helliwell, National Trust tenants and lifelong farmers. But for the transient visitors, it's something else entirely – the main thoroughfare of the Pennine Way.

As the first port of call after the Kinder Scout Plateau, walkers are always stopping at Upper Booth Farm in need of plasters, refreshments or emergency services. But the most useful service provided by Robert and Sarah is a place to crash for the night.

The backdrop to the camping at Upper Booth is spectacular and, like the best countryside campsites, it's difficult to see where the site ends and the open landscape of the Peaks begins. The campsite stretches across two fields. The first, smaller field is flat, sheltered and near to the facilities. The second field is a larger, undulating area of grass, open to expansive Peak District views.

Robert's won awards for achievements on his innovative and environmentally friendly farm. If there was an award for services to walkers, he and Sarah would get that, too.

THE UPSIDE: Peak District views all around from this prime walkers' site.

THE DOWNSIDE: The facilities need updating.

THE DAMAGE: Camping from £4 per person per night; £2 per car; £6 per person per night in the camping barn. No caravans allowed on site.

THE FACILITIES: Flush toilets, a hot shower and washing-up facilities. There's no on-site shop, but you might get a few essentials like milk, eggs and confectionery, if you ask at the farmhouse door.

NEAREST DECENT PUB: From the campsite, it's a half-hour walk along the first (or last) stretch of the Pennine Way to the 'official' start/end point of the path at the historic Old Nag's Head (01433 670291) in Edale village. You might find better food at The Rambler's Inn (p175) down the road.

FOOD AND DRINK: Order one of the site's 'hampers for campers'. Filled with a tasty, locally sourced selection of foods, there's everthing you might want for a weekend. Order when you book.

IF IT RAINS: Head underground to the caves at Castleton (see p175).

TREAT YOURSELF: To some time off your feet and arrange a helicopter ride with Pennine Helis (01457 820152) to survey the scenery from above.

GETTING THERE: Upper Booth Farm is a mile from Edale in the Hope Valley, about 10 miles northeast of Buxton. Follow the signs for Edale from the A625, look out for the signpost to Upper Booth a mile west of the turning for Edale village and station. Follow the road to the end.

OPEN: Mar–Nov.

IF IT'S FULL: The *Cool Camping* site at Fieldhead (p174) is just down the road.

Upper Booth Farm, Upper Booth, nr Edale, Hope Valley, Derbyshire S33 7ZJ

	t	01433 670250	w	www.upperboothcamping.co.uk

jerusalem farm

Camping is all about getting closer to nature, so what better place to camp than in a nature reserve. Jerusalem Farm nestled in the picturesque Luddenden Valley, near Halifax, couldn't be better placed.

Luddenden is a steep and narrow valley, an almost-hidden gorge deep in the heart of Pennine Yorkshire. Luddenden Beck, long exploited by local mills for its fast-flowing waters, runs along its base and it is by the banks of this brook that Jerusalem Farm is sited. As a nature reserve, it's a pristine slice of Pennine perfection, with untouched woods on the surrounding slopes and steep valley walls. For maximum peace and tranquillity, no vehicles are allowed; cars are parked up by reception and equipment carried down to the camping fields.

Visitors are also drawn by the exceptional hill-walking to be found in this region, including the Pennine Way (see p175) and The Calderdale Way (a 50-mile circular walk). You're likely to spot plenty of wildlife on a stroll: much of this area is protected countryside and an important breeding and nesting area for distinctive birds including the curvy-beaked curlew and the splendid, crested lapwing. You'll also see red grouse hopping around wherever there's an abundance of heather.

Take the time to visit this often-overlooked jewel of England's countryside, to scratch beneath the surface, and you'll find yourself strongly attracted to this wild, understated landscape. The call of nature, so to speak.

THE UPSIDE: A car-free riverside campsite at the foot of a small valley.

THE DOWNSIDE: Basic facilities (only one shower) and too many midges (take repellent).

THE DAMAGE: Prices per person per night: adults £5, children £3, under-5s go free. Tents only.

THE FACILITIES: There are toilets, a shower, kids' playground and picnic tables.

NEAREST DECENT PUB: The Cat-I'th-Well (01422 244841) is a great little pub that sells Timothy Taylor's bitter and, curiously for a pub, free-range eggs. It's a half hour walk or a 10-minute drive.

FOOD AND DRINK: You'll get both at the lovely Cat-I'th-Well (see NEAREST DECENT PUB).

IF IT RAINS: Eureka Museum for Children (01422 330069) in Halifax can help keep the little ones entertained. Or for something a bit different, check out the slopes at the Halifax Ski & Snowboard Centre (01422 340760).

TREAT YOURSELF: To a day at the races. York Racecourse (01904 620911) is about an hour away by car.

GETTING THERE: From the A646 at Luddenden Foot turn up Luddenden Lane at the restaurant. After 1½ miles, turn right towards Booth. Go through the village and after the sharp left-hand bend, Jerusalem Lane is 20 metres on the left. Look out for the campsite on the right.

PUBLIC TRANSPORT: The site is a 10-minute walk from the bus terminus at Booth. Or get the train to Halifax, Sowerby Bridge or Hebden Bridge and get a taxi.

OPEN: Easter–Sep.

IF IT'S FULL: Rough Hey Wood Campsite (01422 834586) in Stansfield Mill Lane is just a couple of miles south of Jerusalem Farm.

Jerusalem Farm, Jerusalem Lane, Booth, Halifax, West Yorkshire HX2 6XB	t	01422 883246	f	01422 393276

gordale scar

Wordsworth penned sonnets about it, James Ward painted an enormous canvas of it (now in Tate Britain). And now you can camp in it. Gordale Scar, that massive gaping wound on the skin of Yorkshire's landscape, was hewn 100 metres deep through the limestone rock by successive torrents of glacial meltwater. It now stands as testament to the landscaping force of ice; that single-handed sculptor of Britain's geography.

Sitting humbly at its mouth, dwarfed by the sloping ravine walls, lies Gordale Scar campsite. Out here it feels like you're at the last outpost. The road ends a mile past the campsite and is little more than the farm's driveway. Once you've pitched your tent, you'll feel miniaturised in the face of the scar's sheer cliffs. You couldn't really get any closer, with the scar less than a quarter of a mile away and the pathway leading to its stone face, mere metres from your tent. So, it's an ideal spot to rest weary bones after scrabbling up and down the rock, or simply to enjoy much vertical neck craning.

Though the rumble of the scar's waterfalls are shielded from your ears by the headland, its waters run past the site in the form of Gordale Beck, which splits the site in two. A small flock of the farm's sheep roam freely around the campsite, so watch underfoot for the slippery sheep poo; there's no chance of toilet training them. If you want to escape the daily dodgems, then cross the beck via the stepping stones: the sheep rarely venture over the stream and the water's sounds have a soothing effect come night-time.

You'd be wise to pack your best guide ropes and industrial-strength tent pegs or at least some spares. The breeze can pick up and the narrows of the scar direct the full force of the wind this way, so unless you want your tent to resemble the gnarled and twisted trees on the scar's cliffs, head for the shelter of some hedging or the walls.

The area's a hotbed for climbers looking to conquer the scar and tackle nearby Malham Cove. You can find some satisfaction and a degree of awe by hunkering down and watching others tackling the strenuous verticals from the safety of your fold-out chair. If you do fancy a low-key scrabble of your own then you can clamber up past the tufa-covered rocks beside the falls.

You're not limited to the scar for your entertainment. The Pennine Way, Malham Cove and the thin wispy waterfall of Janet's Foss are a few miles away from the site, so it's ideally placed to pick off some of Yorkshire's icons. A sanctuary from the popularity of the scar can be found in nearby Malham Tarn, which offers a watery retreat and on a calm day mirrors the surrounding woodland and heath in its still waters.

The facilities at Gordale Scar are rudimentary and divide campers. You'll find them in a charming, converted stone barn drenched in ivy; inside it all feels like it was built and last renovated in the Ice Age. It's basic but adequate. However, campers don't come here for the facilities, they come here for the uniquely beautiful Gordale Scar. Being able to camp so close to an English icon should be draw enough for you to stop by. Who knows, it might even inspire you to write your own sonnet.

THE UPSIDE: Rugged and raw camping in iconic English landscape.

THE DOWNSIDE: Quite exposed; at times your tent can get a hurricane-like battering.

THE DAMAGE: For a large tent it's £3 per night, for a small tent £2 per night. Then, it's £3 per person, £2 for a car and £1 for a dog.

THE FACILITIES: These are basic but adequate. There's a 10p charge for hot water from the site's only shower. Fresh water, plus washing-up area.

NEAREST DECENT PUB: The amblers' favourite is The Lister Arms (01729 830 330) in Malham, a 17th-century coaching inn, with fairly decent fare and a selection of independent ales from home and abroad.

FOOD AND DRINK: Treat your stomach to locally grown organic food at Town End Farm Shop (01729 830902) in Airton, with grass-fed beef, lamb and local wines and local micro-brews.

IF IT RAINS: Explore the monastic ruins and food-based diversions of nearby Bolton Abbey (01756 718009).

TREAT YOURSELF: To a ride in the skies on a charter from Pennine Helicopters (01457 820152), based in Saddleworth.

GETTING THERE: From the A65 to Gargrave, take the road towards Malham. Follow signs for the tarn until the road forks, then follow the road to Gordale. The site's 2 miles up on the left.

PUBLIC TRANSPORT: From Skipton take the 210 bus to Malham Buck Inn. From there, go on foot, following signs to Malham Tarn and then at the fork heading towards Gordale. The site's 2 miles up on the left.

OPEN: All year.

IF IT'S FULL: Campsites are few and far between, but the nearby Cool Camping site of Knight Stainforth (p184) offers a quiet rural escape.

Gordale Scar Campsite, Gordale Farm, Malham, North Yorkshire BD23 4DL | t | 01729 830333

knight stainforth

Northern market towns often evoke images of gloomy streets that shut up shop and gave up breathing 20 winters earlier when the coal ran dry. Not so in Settle. Apart from having possibly the most scenic railway station in this fair land, it's also a hive of activity as the main jump-off point for just about every attraction and activity in limestone country.

Situated just outside Settle, overlooking acres of grassy slopes dissected with stone walls and dotted with deserted stone barns, lies Knight Stainforth. Like some kind of campsite divining rod, it too has positioned itself at the confluence of this unseen river of things-to-do.

En route to the site, it seems as if it's a good stretch from anywhere, but it flatters to deceive. The Pennine Way, Cycle way and Bridle way criss-cross just nearby, and many use the site as a stopping-off point.

The dales are littered with many a foss and force and it's almost an obligatory must-do whilst in the area to visit at least one. And you'll not have to venture far from your tent. Bordering the site's edge is Stainforth Force, complete with fairy tale packhorse bridge, although, sadly, no troll.

Here you can sit on the top of the cliff, legs dangling over the plunge pool watching the icy River Ribble tumbling down three tiers of limestone as it heads westwards. It's a tranquil place to rest, and no wonder many set up their tackle and angle away a day or two or four.

For those after a challenge, you can pit your thighs and lungs against those three skyline puncturing peaks – Whernside, Ingleborough and Pen-y-Ghent – all accessible from the site.

If you don't fancy puffing across the moors under your own steam, then catch the famous Settle to Carlisle train. Departing from Settle's picturesque train station, it snakes its way over 45 miles of sumptuous moors scenery and over some of the most back-breaking Victorian engineering works, ranking as one of Britain's finest train journeys.

The site itself is a bit of a looker. Its flat expanse is finely manicured and gazes up to country hills at either side. The generously sized pitches can comfortably house even the new-breed super-size family tents and with two large fields, you'll be certain to find some grass to call your own.

The site does attract a fair few caravans and can become slightly swamped, but they receive no preferential treatment and tenters are not seen as second-class citizens. That said, the caravans have led to the inclusion of security barriers and swipe cards, which whilst making for a safe environment, takes a bit of the fun out of it. And the question of whether you need wi-fi when you're out camping is debatable, too. Whatever your take on it, the site's been running for 80 years and has regulars that have been gracing its pastures for over 50 years. And, they say numbers don't lie.

The facilities can't be knocked. In addition to a high-quality amenities block, an encyclopedic information booth helps you make the most of the area and an extensively stocked on-site shop sells maps, food and ale, as well as locally raised Hellifield Highlander beef.

If the weather turns, then nearby Skipton can offer you fortress-like sanctuary from the outdoors in its 12th-century castle, and the town is brimming with market stalls. It's worth hanging around to catch the downtime between groups of coach parties that regularly stop here on their flying visits.

Whatever your plans in this nexus of attractions, Knight Stainforth is a great base-camp to take on a mountain of things to do in the area.

THE UPSIDE: Friendly, family focused site.

THE DOWNSIDE: It's a bit too slick and organised here; the security barrier is a bit of overkill. And the caravan count can be high.

THE DAMAGE: £12 per night for a tent, 2 people and a car. £2 for electric hook-up. Extra adults (17 and over) cost £2.50 and extra kids (5–16) £1.50.

THE FACILITIES: There's a children's playground, free hot showers, washing-up room, games room, wi-fi and a small shop selling fundamentals, walking maps and alcohol.

NEAREST DECENT PUB: The Craven Heifer Hotel (01729 822599), a 10-minute walk from the site up a steep lane, is the furthest you can possibly find from a trendy gastropub and sports interesting 1980s-style décor. However, it sells local ales, reasonably priced home-made food and the beer garden overlooks the local beck.

FOOD AND DRINK: Chomp down on locally raised Hellifield Highland beef from the campsite's shop. Settle also holds farmer's markets every second Sunday of the month.

IF IT RAINS: Escape the deluge underground in White Scar Cave (01524 241244), England's largest cave and a subterranean world of waterfalls and luminous stalagtites.

TREAT YOURSELF: To a mineral soak and a massage at The Devonshire Arms' spa (01756 710411) near Bolton Abbey. And if you have time, check out its Michelin-starred restaurant.

OPEN: Mar–Oct.

GETTING THERE: Leave the A65 at Settle and take the B6479 through to Giggleswick. Turn right onto Stackhouse Lane. Follow the narrow lane for about 2 miles, the site is signposted on your right at the crossroads.

PUBLIC TRANSPORT: Get yourself to Settle, take the 581 bus, jumping off in Little Stainforth. The site is signposted from the crossroads.

IF IT'S FULL: The *Cool Camping* site at Gordale Scar (p180) is just half an hour's drive away.

Knight Stainforth, Little Stainforth, Settle, North Yorkshire BD24 0DP

| | t | 01729 822200 | w | www.knightstainforth.fsnet.co.uk |

spiers house

Let's start with the facts. Spiers House campsite is one of the best campsites owned and run by the Forestry Commission. It's situated in the heart of Cropton Forest about 20 miles west of Scarborough in the North Yorks Moors National Park. But what the facts don't tell you is what an amazing area this is for a varied and active holiday.

The main thing to remember before setting off for Spiers House is to pack a mountain bike. And if you've got children, make sure they've got theirs too. When you turn off the public highway towards Spiers House you travel along a long, winding driveway that takes you deep into the forest. The setting is undeniably pretty, with all the feeling of a remote, magical woodland. All around are miles of hassle-free, traffic-free (but not effort-free!) cycling within Cropton Forest.

If mundane matters such as the standard of site facilities bother you, then worry not. It's efficiently run with excellent facilities and a very handy shop – a necessity for a campsite so remotely situated.

Whilst the biking is exceptional, there is one standard tourist attraction that should not be missed. The North Yorkshire Moors Steam Railway, which puffs and chugs its way between Pickering and Grosmont.

But the main event has to be the biking. Up on the moors above Rosedale is an off-road biking route that cannot be bettered anywhere in Britain. It's a hard day's cycling for us mortals, but such is the stuff of true adventure, of which there are plentiful opportunities from Spiers House.

THE UPSIDE: Fantastic off-road biking opportunities all around. Beautifully situated for a tranquil, hassle-free holiday.

THE DOWNSIDE: A long way from the shops – and beware of the midges!

THE DAMAGE: Tent and 2 people £8.70–11.50 per night (weekdays), rising to £9.80–12 at weekends. Extra people (over 5) are £3.50–4.80.

THE FACILITIES: Very good, with toilets, hot showers, family room, disabled facilities, laundry, washing-up sinks and children's play area. On-site shop sells food, maps, gas refills and a few camping accessories.

NEAREST DECENT PUB: No pub for miles!

FOOD AND DRINK: PYO fruit at Cedar Barn (01751 475614), which is about 8 miles away.

IF IT RAINS: Plenty on offer around here. The North Yorkshire Moors Railway (01751 472508) is a lovely day out. The bright lights of Scarborough are also within easy reach. Castle Howard (01653 648444) is impressive and worthwhile; for non-cyclists there is Dalby Forest Drive (01751 472771). For something different, visit the Cropton Brewery (01751 417330).

TREAT YOURSELF: To a high-wire adventure at Go Ape in Dalby Forest (0845 6439215).

GETTING THERE: From the A170 (Thirsk to Scarborough) 2 miles before Pickering, at the village of Wrelton, take the minor road signposted to Rosedale Abbey, then a mile beyond Cropton, turn right into the forest, signposted for the site.

PUBLIC TRANSPORT: In high season only you can catch the Moorbus service to the site from Pickering, which operates three times a day.

OPEN: Apr–Jan; open only from May in 2008 due to refurbishment.

IF IT'S FULL: Another recommended campsite within easy reach is Rosedale Camping Park at Rosedale Abbey (01751 417272).

Spiers House Campsite, Cropton Forest, Cropton, Pickering, North Yorkshire YO18 8ES

| t | 0845 130 8224 | w | www.forestholidays.co.uk |

hooks house farm

Robin Hoods Bay, near Whitby in North Yorkshire, is an area steeped in romance and intrigue. Its very name is a mystery: there's nothing to link this place with the infamous hero of Sherwood Forest, but the name stands as an inexplicable suggestion of some legendary past.

What's certain is that this was smuggler country. Throughout the 18th century, locals crippled by high taxes turned to smuggling to make money, receiving tobacco, brandy, rum and silk from Holland and France. Gangs of smugglers used a network of underground passages and secret tunnels to deliver the stash inland, making a tidy profit in the process.

Even now, the charming town of Robin Hoods Bay, also known locally as Bay Town, or simply Bay, has the feel of an age-old smugglers' den, with unfeasibly narrow streets and tight passageways. Ancient fishermen's cottages cling to a near-vertical slope as the cliff drops down to a little fishing harbour at the water's edge. In addition to the older part of town on the side of the cliff, there's a newer enclave on the flat ground at the top. The well-ordered Victorian mansions are a world apart from the cobbled jumble below.

It has to be said, Robin Hoods Bay, although picturesque, doesn't have a 'lie-on-the-sand' beach. The ground at the foot of the bay is dark and rocky, more suitable for bracing walks, exploring rock pools and fossil-hunting than sunbathing. But the wide sweep of bay is stunning. And a great vantage point from which to enjoy this vista is at Hooks House Farm campsite on the hill above the town.

Hooks House Farm is a friendly, family-run campsite occupying a grassy field that slopes gently down towards the bay. The first-rate views really make this site: from here you can watch the tide wash in and out over the whole sweep of the bay and beyond. The campsite vibe is peaceful, relaxed and low-key, with no organised entertainment and no long list of rules and regulations to adhere to. The site is next to a road, but as the road isn't inundated with vehicles you're more likely to be bothered by sheep bleating in the nearby fields than by traffic noise.

The owners, Jill and Gordon Halder, are famously attentive, ensuring that all facilities are kept suitably clean and that all visitors have everything they need. The facilities are adequate rather than exceptional, with two showers in each of the prefab amenities blocks, although there are plans to double this capacity. Extra services include stables for hire on this working farm, so you can even bring your horse on holiday.

With the Yorkshire Moors within striking distance, the countryside is perfect for walking and cycling as well as horse riding. The disused railway line that runs through here on its way from Scarborough to Whitby has been transformed into a popular walking and cycling path, and it forms part of the wittily-named Moor to Sea cycle path, a long-distance route that provides up to four days of cycling. Robin Hoods Bay also marks the eastern end of the classic Coast to Coast Walk from St Bees Head, a superb two-week walk taking in three National Parks: The Lake District, The Yorkshire Dales and the North Yorkshire Moors.

If it's shorter walks you're after, try the half-mile stretch along a country path to Robin Hoods Bay village and its selection of five pubs, all great venues for discussing the demise of smuggling as a lucrative career, for the possibility of finding fossils on the beach and for speculating how Robin Hoods Bay might have found its name.

THE UPSIDE: Panoramic bay views and easy walks.

THE DOWNSIDE: Light sleepers might be affected by slight traffic and sheep noise.

THE DAMAGE: From £5 per adult per night and £2 per child, £3 extra for electric hook-up.

THE FACILITIES: There are showers, toilets, disabled toilet and washroom, kitchen, stables and electric hook-ups.

NEAREST DECENT PUB: Of the five pubs in town, our favourite is The Dolphin (01947 880337) for its cosy old-world smugglers' feel, but The Bay Hotel (01947 880278), right down by the quayside, has sea views.

FOOD AND DRINK: In Whitby's Old Fire Hall you'll find the weekly farmer's market every Wednesday between May and October.

IF IT RAINS: The busy fishing harbour of Whitby, some 5 miles to the north, deserves investigation. Attractions include Whitby Abbey and the Captain Cook Museum (01947 601900).

TREAT YOURSELF: To some canoeing or rowing on the River Esk with Ruswarp Pleasure Boats (01947 604658) near Whitby.

GETTING THERE: Heading south from Whitby on the A171, take the B1447 signposted to Robin Hoods Bay. Hooks House Farm is on the right, half a mile before the village.

PUBLIC TRANSPORT: Arriva buses from Scarborough to Middlesbrough run through Robin Hoods Bay and Whitby. Buses stop at the campsite gate's year round.

OPEN: All year.

IF IT'S FULL: More sea views can be had from Bay Ness Farm (www.baynessfarm.co.uk). They only accept campers who have booked in advance via the Internet.

Hooks House Farm, Whitby Road, Robin Hoods Bay, North Yorkshire YO22 4PE

| | t | 01947 880283 | w | www.hookshousefarm.co.uk |

la rosa

Day-glo carnival psychedelia is the order of the day at La Rosa, where camping and the world of kitsch go colourfully and surreally hand in hand. Here, you can lose yourself inside one of eight retro-vintage camper vans from the 1920s and the 1960s, each individually and lovingly furnished from flea-markets, second-hand stores, bric-a-brac, vintage shops and eBay. Camp? That's an understatement, darling!

Each trailer has its own kitsch theme. In Tinkers' Trailer you can spend the night as a gypsy; or bow to The King in the reflective American-style Elvis trailer. Go on a night's Seventies Safari or on a trip with Barbara Cartland on acid in Psycho Candy. Whichever you end up in, you'll never have stayed anywhere quite like it.

The four camper vans in the bottom field have wood-burning stoves to keep you sauna-like warm during the night. Bedding, a nightly supply of wood, gas and near limitless candles to light your way come sundown are all provided. And once you're snug inside your caravan of kitsch, grab one of the hand-picked books and educate yourself on that burlesque icon Betty Page in the Gypsy Rosa Lee trailer, or uncover Romany culture in Tinkers.

And did we mention the circus big top? This large communal tent, built by a real circus actor, sits atop a grove in the top field surrounded by green, 1920s, UK-made camper vans. Inside there's a large communal area and kitchen, not to mention the fancy dress rail, just in case you want to totally immerse yourself in this world of fantasy.

If the carnival of chintz isn't enough to escape from reality, then the setting can only ease a troubled mind. The site is hemmed in on all sides by the North Yorkshire Moors Park forest and has views from the lower field out over this beautiful, expansive moorland. When night descends, you'll have to navigate the campsite by a runway of tea-lights. And if you're lucky enough to have a camper van with a stove, the nights in front of your hearth lit only by candlelight will be cosy.

The campness even extends to your daily ablutions, which take place in a pre-war shepherd's hut, decked out like a circus clairvoyants'. The shower is outside in a converted milking parlour, complete with wind-up record player and vintage LP collection for the ultimate shower singing experience.

Outside of La Rosa, you'll find several references to popular culture within the local area. Nearby Goathland is better known to millions as *Heartbeat*'s Aidensfield and you can wander its streets exploring the sights of Yorkshire's infamous time warp soap. Goathland's train station also doubled as the Hogwarts station in the Harry Potter films but if you want to see the real deal then the North Yorkshire Moors Railway's steam trains chug in and out as if from a bygone era.

Dracula's drop-off point in the UK, Whitby, is only 9 short miles away, looked over by its iconic Abbey. If the gothic vampire doesn't get your heart racing, take the 199 steps to the top of the ruins for some sure-fire blood-pumping action. Or you can opt for (supposedly) the best fish and chips in the land; plus, there's fresh mussels, cockles and all manner of seafood to satisfy any cravings.

A day out in the real world of Yorkshire might seem a bit monotone after the extraordinary radioactive colour of La Rosa. But as the time to return to your trailer nears and you utter the words, 'back to camp', never will they have sounded more appropriate.

THE UPSIDE: One-of-a-kind camping in kitsch caravans and trailers.

THE DOWNSIDE: For all the lure, chintz and charm, the facilities may be too basic for some.

THE DAMAGE: £27 per person per night; price includes bedding, gas, candles and fire wood. In July and August there's a 2-night minimum stay.

THE FACILITIES: There's no electricity in the camper vans, but 4 have wood-burning stoves. There's a communal kitchen in the big top, a washing area and a free shower.

NEAREST DECENT PUB: One of England's oldest, and eccentric pubs, The Birch Hall Inn (01947 896245) in Beckhole serves 'Beckhole butties' with a range of local micro-brews, all available through the tiny hatchway of a bar.

FOOD AND DRINK: You can't get fish much fresher than this. There's over 120 species of off-the-boat fish available for your stove at The Whitby Catch (01947 601313) on Pier Road.

IF IT RAINS: Stay in, light the wood-burning stove and read a book.

TREAT YOURSELF: Think Orient Express and dine in style on the North Yorkshire Moors Railway (01751 472508) inside classic trains and carriages.

GETTING THERE: Take the A64, then the A169 to Pickering. In Goathland, follow the Egton Bridge Roman Road for 2½ miles then turn right. You'll see red flowers on the gatepost after you turn.

PUBLIC TRANSPORT: Take the train to Goathland, and walk into Beck Hole, then up the pathway through the woods. Call for detailed directions.

OPEN: Mar–mid-Oct.

IF IT'S FULL: Walk-ins are guaranteed disappointment. Abbots House Farm in Goathland (01947 896270) is 2½ miles away in a tree-lined site set back from the village.

La Rosa Campsite Extraordinaire, Murk Esk Cottage, Goathland, Whitby, North Yorkshire YO22 5AS

| | t | 07786 072866 | w | www.larosa.co.uk |

highside farm

In times gone by, camping food was limited to tins of beans and packets of soup. The simple sausage was considered the height of culinary innovation. But thanks to celebrity chefs and a million cookbooks, everyone now knows how to handle a frying pan, and as a result, cooking at camp has become as adventurous as Heston Blumenthal. And for those of you who treat a camping trip as an excuse to seek out fresh, local produce, Highside Farm should be high on your list.

Sitting atop the Northern Pennines, the farm's small-holding has only 10 pitches, so its miniature size almost guarantees you'll have plenty of peace and quiet. Staring out over the valley to Lunedale and Teesdale, the extensive views from your tent are sure to whet your appetite.

Dribbling continues when you discover that the site's owners – Richard and Stephanie – also run a working farm, specialising in raising Teeswater sheep and Shorthorn cattle. Both these rare breeds once covered the area 100 years ago, but are now nearly non-existent in the British Isles.

And what the farm sows, you can reap. All the farm-produced meat is available for your campsite stove and for your dining pleasure. And, when the chickens aren't on strike, or off squabbling around the campsite, there's fresh eggs to be had, too. You might need to improvise, as what's in the pantry depends on the season. But, whatever it is, it's guaranteed to be just what your taste buds have been looking for, and a far cry from what your palette may be used to from the weekly supermarket run.

If cooking sounds like way too much effort, then you can simply place an order for breakfast the next day. Anything from bacon sandwiches to a Full English can be rustled up come morning by Richard and Stephanie. This couple certainly know a thing or two about service and do their utmost for their guests: greeting new arrivals with coffee, tea and biscuits after hearing the rumble of a car on the drive, if you're expected.

The food trail continues beyond the campsite, and you can sniff out more local specialities, from pigeon to venison, in several pubs in the area. Copperstone cheese produced by a local dairy can also be bought in the town, so you'll be able to stock up and take the tantalising flavours of Middleton-in-Teesdale home with you.

If all this fattening talk doesn't have you looking for the nearest chaise longue, then any post-binge guilt can be worked off along the Pennine Way, or by heading out to stare into Cauldron Snout. Or if you're convalescing after an intake of good food, more sedate pleasures can be had looking out over the crashing tumble of High Force, Britain's largest waterfall. The area is a hotbed for canoeists, who can often be seen weaving and wending their way down river and over the falls further down at Lower Force.

The nearby town of Barnard Castle offers nothing more strenuous than moving your pupils as you roam around the French *château*-like Bowes Museum, and its large collection of fine art.

When Richard and Stephanie bought the farm, they wanted to create a campsite that was true to what they loved about camping. No security barriers, packed-out camping fields, rules, regulations or keycodes. Just good views, a rural setting, nice walks and that back-to-nature feeling. And the added ingredient of good-quality local food. Now, that sounds like a recipe for success.

THE UPSIDE: Miniature rural site.

THE DOWNSIDE: Without a generous dusting of DEET, you'll be eaten alive.

THE DAMAGE: £7 per person per night, and under-3s go free. Electric hook-up £2.50.

THE FACILITIES: The single shower with free hot water and a solitary toilet sit inside a traditional farm building, just to add to the charm.

NEAREST DECENT PUB: Being on the edge of civilisation it's 2 miles to the nearest pub. The Blacksmith Arms (01833 640605) in Mickleton and Three Tuns Inn (01833 650 289) in Eggleston both serve local food with a village atmosphere.

FOOD AND DRINK: In addition to the seasonal offerings at Highside Farm, grab yourself some local Cotherstone cheese, named after a village in Teesdale. It's available from the farmer's market (the first Saturday of the month) or from Armitages (01833 690909) in Middleton-in-Teesdale.

IF IT RAINS: Seek refuge in the keep at Barnard Castle (01833 638212) or the nearby Bowes Museum (01833 690606).

GETTING THERE: Take the A685 towards Brough. Then take the B6276, the site is 2 miles from Middleton-in-Teesdale on your right.

PUBLIC TRANSPORT: No chance. But book in advance and you can rustle a pick-up from Middleton-in-Teesdale.

OPEN: Apr–Sep.

IF IT'S FULL: Farmyard camping and cooking can be found at Farmhouse Kitchen (01833 640506), 5 miles away off the road to Middleton-in-Teesdale. Just follow the brown campsite signs.

Highside Farm, Bowbank, Middleton-in-Teesdale, County Durham DL12 0NT

| | t | 01833 640135 | w | www.highsidefarm.co.uk |

gibraltar farm

Morecambe Bay is a big landscape in little old England. The sweeping bay stretches for miles along the northwest coast, with an extended shoreline taking in villages and towns from Fleetwood to Barrow-in-Furness, a road trip of about 70 miles. This landscape is beautiful and dangerous. On a hot Bank Holiday with the tide out and kids playing in the golden sand, it's an innocent summer delight. But the sand holds hidden dangers. Many a cockle-picker or sand-walking traveller have been trapped by the fast rising tide, and not all have survived to tell the tale.

One of the best places from which to enjoy the sands is at Gibraltar Farm campsite, near Silverdale. The camping area lies at the back of the farm. The access road takes you down through a lovely, terraced caravan field and, beyond the trees, to the tent field – a large grassy area set around a rocky protrusion. The waters of Morecambe Bay can be seen just beyond the low wall.

Less than a mile away from the campsite is Jenny Brown's Point, a popular viewpoint and bird-watching spot overlooking the bay. And the nearby RSPB reserve at Leighton Moss offers access to coastal lagoons, nature trials, hides and a Visitor Centre.

Aside from the birds, Morecambe is famous for two other reasons. The first is Eric Morecambe, the comedian and one half of Morecambe and Wise. The second is cockle-picking. Anyone can pick cockles, just be sure to take advice about the tides. It pays to be wise in Morecambe.

THE UPSIDE: Farm camping with bay views.

THE DOWNSIDE: The warden needs to stamp down on late-night party noise.

THE DAMAGE: Tent with 1/2/4 people is £5/8/10; caravan without/with electric hook-up is £9/12. No charge for cars or awnings.

THE FACILITIES: Flush toilets, washing-up area, electric hook-ups; only one male and one female shower, so expect to queue. Home-made ice creams from the shop. Supplies are available in nearby Silverdale, but for a better choice of shops go to Arnside, where there's also a post office.

NEAREST DECENT PUB: The Silverdale Hotel (01524 701206) in the village is less than a mile away but, aside from a pleasant beer garden, isn't very inspiring. There are some better pubs in Arnside, about 3 miles away, where The Albion (01524 761226) has a waterside beer garden, real ales and an interesting menu.

FOOD AND DRINK: Grab yourself some chops or steaks to slap on the BBQ from Poteau & Son Continental Butchers (01524 761217) in Arnside.

IF IT RAINS: Check out the Wolfhouse Gallery (01524 701405) almost opposite the campsite. It displays paintings, ceramics and jewellery. Its café is good and serves light lunches, tea and cakes.

TREAT YOUSELF: To some potted shrimps from Morecambe Bay; James Baxter & Son (01524 410910) in Morecambe have been potting shrimps for over 200 years.

GETTING THERE: Silverdale is about 11 miles southwest of Kendal. From the A6, take the B5282 to Arnside, then follow the signs to Silverdale. Go through the village, then follow Hollins Lane for less than a mile; as the road turns sharply to the left, Gibraltar Farm is on the right.

PUBLIC TRANSPORT: Take the train to Silverdale and catch the shuttle bus to the site.

OPEN: Apr–Oct.

IF IT'S FULL: There are more sea views from the rough-and-ready campsite at Hollins Farm (01524 701767) in Far Arnside.

Gibraltar Farm Campsite, Hollins Lane, Silverdale, Lancashire LA5 0AU | t | 01524 701736 | w | www.gibraltarfarm.co.uk

full circle

Let's face it, Mongolia is a long way to go camping. And if the 20,000-mile round trip out to the desolate steppes sounds a trite too far for that night in a yurt camping experience, then look no further. Full Circle is camping with a round twist.

For the uninitiated, a yurt is a traditional home of the nomadic tribes that eke out their eon-old existence in the steppes of East and Central Asia, from Iran to Mongolia. Essentially it is a wooden-lattice framed circular tent that supports a conical roof. Historically they'd be covered in animal hide and traditional folk designs, able to withstand the –50°C temperatures the nomads have to contend with.

Thankfully, you'll not have to endure such harsh extremes. Full Circle's yurts sport their own wood-burning stove and with the massive log pile provided it'll be like a Scandinavian sweat lodge come nightfall.

These yurts are the real deal. Shipped in from the steppes, they're crafted by a yurt maker in Ulaan Baatar, each one intricately and ornately decorated with traditional designs. Inside, it's not as spartan as those that Genghis and his hordes would have decamped to after a hard day's pillaging.

Each yurt has a rug-covered wooden floor, and comfy double and single beds; they can sleep a tribe up to six comfortably with its reserve of blow-up mattresses.

A large supply of candles, tea-lights, a small stove and armoury of cooking equipment, board games and books mean that once you're in, you'll never actually have to leave until your stay comes to an end. And that's part of the ethos behind the camping here at Full Circle. Whilst at home we live our separate lives in our own quarter of our home, here whole families and friends enjoy communal living.

Where the wooden slats of the yurt come together a small, jigsaw-like circular window stares skywards. Come night-time, you can lie back, watch the fire dance on the walls from your toasty bed and stare out at the starry lights above, or just listen out for the bark of deer in the woods.

Each yurt is set idyllically amongst the woodlands surrounding nearby Rydall Beck, looking down the hillside with the faint sliver of Windermere sometimes visible on the horizon. Within earshot, Rydal Beck rumbles its way through the woods; a pathway at the back of the site follows the river up into the hills, past its endless falls, torrents, plunge pools and weirs, all the way to Rydal Water.

But you needn't go so far to escape into the surrounding green. There's always Rydal Hall's 30-acre woodland to explore, enough to keep you occupied for a week, with its sculptures and its 600-year-old sweet chestnut tree, as well as the international additions of towering redwoods and Japanese maples. Rydal Hall was home to Wordsworth's landlady, Lady de Fleming, and you can follow in the wordsmith's footsteps up to Rydal Mount, Loughrigg or Grasmere Valley and the many other walks accessible from the Hall.

Whilst this may not be Mongolia, come day's end when you're staring up at the night sky as the wood crackles in the hearth, it'll at least feel like you're a million miles from home.

THE UPSIDE: Unique living in the round.

THE DOWNSIDE: There are only 3 yurts, so book in advance.

THE DAMAGE: Yurts cost £230–260 for a short break; weekly stays between £340 and £410.

THE FACILITIES: Shared with Rydal Hall's campsite, there are hot showers, a washing-up area, running water and an adventure playground for the kids.

NEAREST DECENT PUB: Set in the 17th-century coaching house of Glen Rothay Hotel, Badgers Bar (01539 434500) offers locally sourced food, washed down with local ales around the open fire. There's often local bands playing, too.

FOOD AND DRINK: Check out the UK's first wholly organic wine shop, Organico (01539 431122) in Ambleside. This traditional family business sources and stocks local and international vine produce.

IF IT RAINS: Fire up the hearth, grab a book and listen to the pitter-patter from your cosy haven. If you want to get out and about, just nip down to Wordsworth's Rydal Hall, which lies within the grounds and Ambleside's only a short drive away.

TREAT YOURSELF: Get all J. R. Hartley and head to Esthwaite Water Trout Fishery (01539 436541), in Hawkshead, for a spot of fly-fishing. You can just buy a permit or get instruction, whichever suits.

GETTING THERE: Follow the A591 into Rydal and then follow signs for Rydal Hall. In the grounds stay on the track to the right, over the bridge and through the gate. Go up the steep track to the parking area.

PUBLIC TRANSPORT: Catch the 599 bus from Windermere train station, getting off at Rydal Church. Then, walk up the hill to the Hall. Follow the track through the gate and up the hill.

OPEN: Easter–Dec.

IF IT'S FULL: Camping is also available in the wooded grounds of Rydal Hall (01539 432050).

Full Circle, Rydal Hall, Ambleside, Cumbria LA22 9LX | t | 01539 821278 | w | www.lake-district-yurts.co.uk

low wray

Low Wray National Trust campsite sits on the quieter western shore of Lake Windermere. It's a small site with two main areas for camping; one set back from the lake in a clearing surrounded by trees, and another tree-scattered spot right on the shore with expansive views across the water. Without a doubt, the tiny lakeside site is the best place to pitch, despite the £5 surcharge and the longer walk from the car (vehicles must be parked in the designated areas, away from the camping grass).

A night or two camping at this lakeside location is unforgettable. In the early evening, the sunlight dances through the tall trees to light up the BBQ smoke; and if the weather stays to give a decent sunrise over the lake, it can feel like the most restful place on earth.

As you would expect from a National Trust site, it's well-organised with good facilities. You also need to make sure you're fully provisioned as the small campsite shop doesn't open for long, and when it does, there's not much to buy.

Aside from the great location next to England's largest lake and the possibilities for sailing, kayaking and fishing, the campsite is well-positioned to take in some of the Lake District's 'dry' attractions. There are plenty of opportunities for walking and off-road cycling, with paths leading directly from the campsite. This is also Beatrix Potter country, so a trip here wouldn't be complete without visiting either her home at Hill Top near Sawrey or the Beatrix Potter Gallery in Hawkshead, which houses an exhibition of her original paintings.

THE UPSIDE: Unforgettable lakeside camping – if you can bag one of the few spots! Turn up promptly at 1pm when reception opens.

THE DOWNSIDE: The midges – take repellent.

THE DAMAGE: Adult £4.50–5.50, child £2–2.50 and a family rate of £11–13.50 per night. Vehicles are £3–3.50 and there's a lakeside premium of £5 per tent. Tents only.

THE FACILITIES: Shop, laundry, kids' playground, hot showers, disabled facilities, boat launching. Vehicles must be parked off the camping grass.

NEAREST DECENT PUB: It's not that near (a 10-minute drive or 40-minute walk) but The Drunken Duck Inn (01539 436347) near Ambleside is one of England's best pubs with an award-winning restaurant and ales brewed on site.

FOOD AND DRINK: Wander around Ambleside and visit the foody-fantastic world of Lucy's Specialist Grocers (01539 432223).

IF IT RAINS. Grab some popcorn and see a film at Zeffirelli's Cinema (015394 33845) in Ambleside.

TREAT YOURSELF: To a room at the excellent Drunken Duck Inn if it's really chucking it down.

GETTING THERE: From Ambleside, take the A593 to Clappersgate then turn left onto the B5286. Turn left again at the sign for Wray, the site is less than a mile on the left.

PUBLIC TRANSPORT: The Coniston ramber bus from Ambleside to Windermere takes you within a mile of the site.

OPEN: Easter–Oct.

IF IT'S FULL: The Great Langdale NT Campsite (01539 437668) is just up the road, as is the Cool Camping pick Baysbrown Farm (p210).

Low Wray National Trust Campsite, Low Wray, nr Ambleside, Cumbria LA22 0JA

t	01539 432810	w	www.nationaltrust.org.uk

baysbrown farm

The Lakes. Adjectives can't do the landscape justice. And nor can the expletives, when summer tourists gridlock the roads. But there is some respite from the mayhem – at the lake-free valley of Great Langdale, near Ambleside, that seems to escape the worst of the crowds. Sitting serenely in the heart of the valley is Baysbrown Farm, which nestles up against a steep fell on one side, and on the other looks out over three generously sized camping fields that gently slope down to the valley's river.

The site lies beneath the humbling rocks of Crinkle Crags, Bowfell and the Langdale Pikes, that all seem to swallow up your tent, the farmhouse and the distant village, giving a sense of scale rarely found in the Lakes. Peering out from your tent each morning at the mist-shrouded peaks is worth the entrance money alone.

You and your tent will be at the heart of the farm, surrounded on all sides by 800 acres. Baying floats over the lichen-drenched walls from the farm's resident flock of Herdwick sheep, which look quizzically out at you from the adjacent field. Chickens run amok around your guide ropes, much to the kids' delight and farm machinery rumbles along the lane. Life here just seems slower and simpler.

And it is. The site doesn't have any designated spots; just rock up and pitch where you like. And with the site's size it's easy to find your own corner of peace and tranquillity. Then, when you're done, just walk up to the farmhouse and holler your arrival into the ever-open kitchen door and hand over your fee. There's no such thing as booking in advance here; it's just not that kind of place.

Plenty of pathways criss-cross the valley by the farm. You can go all-expeditionary onto the Langdale Pikes and ascend Pavey Ark or Pike of Stickle. Or opt for easier targets, following the undulating river along the valley floor or heading up to the idyllic Elterwater. The bridle paths in the valley make for good, suspension-testing cycle routes, and many mountain bikers use the farm as a base.

However you've worked up that salty brow by day end, nourishment and that well-earned pint can be found at Chapel Stiles' sole watering hole – Wainwrights' Inn. If all the valley's frolicking lambs haven't caused you to question your carnivorous cravings, then try their infamous, overly generous portion of lamb shoulder. Despite Baysbrown being a working farm, there's no produce available to throw onto the gas stove, although a short amble to the café in Chapel Stile can fill your larder with the basics.

The near-endless activities, sights and museums in and around nearby Ambleside and Windermere (a mere 20-minute drive away), make Baysbrown Farm an ideal refuge once the day's explorations in the tourist hot-spots are done with. Come night-time Bruce, the farmer, likes to maintain the silence so there's no-nonsense and no-noise after 10.30pm. And it's almost like the rest of the valley heeds this imposed watershed, too, bar the odd hoot of an owl or baa from a sheep, as the night air is filled only with the rustle of your tent in the breeze.

If you're after a quiet rural escape from a case of Lakes-induced hydrophobia, then the lake-free Langdale valley is where you'll find it. In the seclusion of the farm grounds and the shelter of the dale, you'll be twiddling reeds between your teeth without a care in no time.

THE UPSIDE: The simple life in the heart of the dale.

THE DOWNSIDE: No advanced bookings.

THE DAMAGE: Adults cost £4 per person per night; children (5–16) are £2 and under-5s free.

THE FACILITIES: There are free hot showers, 2 toilet blocks (one quite basic and the other newly built) and a washing-up area.

NEAREST DECENT PUB: Wainwrights' Inn (01539 438088) serves up Real Jennings and home-brewed Wainwright Ale with healthy servings of decent food.

FOOD AND DRINK: The Drunken Duck Inn (01539 436 347) near Ambleside sets off salivary glands with its gastronomic menu and views out over tarns and craggy fells.

IF IT RAINS: Indulge the kids (or take a nostalgic trip back to childhood stories) at The World of Beatrix Potter Attraction (015394 88444) in Bowness-on-Windermere. Plus, Windermere and Ambleside with their hosts of tea rooms, shops, museums and other indoor pursuits are only a 20-minute drive away.

TREAT YOURSELF: Escape to refinement at Gilpin Lodge (015394 88818). This fell-based country house near Windermere dishes up Michelin-rated delights (they have 1 star) amongst its private 20 acres. Rooms range from £125 to £180 per person per night.

GETTING THERE: Take the A591 to Ambleside. From the town centre follow the B5343 to Chapel Stile. The campsite is signposted on the right a mile past Wainwrights' Inn.

PUBLIC TRANSPORT: Get yourself to Ambleside and take the 'Langdale Rambler' (bus 516) to Chapel Stile. Disembark at Brambles Café, the campsite is signposted on the right ¼ mile further down the road.

OPEN: Mar–Oct.

IF IT'S FULL: A good option is Great Langdale National Trust campsite (01539 437 668) 2 miles further up the road.

Baysbrown Farm, Great Langdale, Ambleside, Cumbria LA22 9JZ | t | 01539 437150

turner hall farm

If you're looking for a truly remote, wilderness camping experience, you'd find it hard to do much better than Turner Hall Farm in the Lake District's lesser-visited Duddon Valley. The reality is, it's not that far from civilisation, but it feels like the middle of nowhere, given the journey there.

The most spectacular way to arrive at Turner Hall Farm is to drive over the Wrynose Pass, a tortuous zigzag of a road, often single-track, frequently hairpinned and always threatening to throw your car down the steep sides of the hill with one wrong move. It's an exhilarating drive that matches some of the best Lake District walks, view for view. If you're a nervous driver, take the safer long, winding road via Broughton Mills. Even from here, you have to get out of the car to open and close gates, an action loaded with the symbolism of leaving civilisation behind.

Turner Hall Farm is tucked into the folds of the fells between the mountains of Scafell Pike to the northwest, and the Old Man of Coniston to the southeast. It's a basic campsite for walkers and climbers, the attraction being its location and outlook rather than the facilities. But the surrounding fells provide an unforgettable backdrop that makes for a fine, inspiring vista. It's a raw, boulder-strewn, long-grassed site, with private corners for sheltered pitching in amongst the crags and drystone walls. Weathered and worn, beaten and torn, the site merges as one into the rugged fell landscape. It's all pretty low-key for a campsite: just turn up, pitch your tent and you might or might not be charged in the morning. There's no reception or shop, but it's a short walk to the pub, and a longer walk to the local post office and general stores.

Campers at Turner Hall Farm are invariably here to walk, with hikes to the lofty peaks of Scafell Pike and The Old Man of Coniston high on the list. These are challenging treks for energetic walkers, but you can warm up with one of the easier walks that criss-cross these fells, taking in lower-altitude pikes, tarns, crags and waterfalls. Popular routes include hiking over the Dunnerdale Fells into the charming, untouched Lickle Valley, home of the age-old Blacksmiths Arms watering hole, or across Birker Fell and down into Eskdale where a steam railway and the historic, supposedly haunted Muncaster Castle provide some family attractions.

A short walk across the fields from the campsite lies the Walna Scar track, one of the oldest roads in the Lake District. In times gone by, it was used by packhorses weighed down with copper ore from the mines at Coniston, and by carts carrying stone from the nearby quarries. It's long-established as a walker's highway, too, linking the Dunnerdale Fells with the Old Man of Coniston and leading on to the town of Coniston itself. It's now also popular with mountain bikers, happy to endure the tough, bike-carrying uphill sections for the adrenaline-pumping downhills. Off-road vehicles also ply some sections of this track, although erosion intermittently forces the National Trust to ban this activity.

Turner Hall Farm may be as off the beaten track as you can get, but thankfully you don't need a 4x4 to get there. Just remember to shut the gates behind you as you leave civilisation.

THE UPSIDE: A glorious wilderness amongst rocky crags and famous fells.

THE DOWNSIDE: Now the facilities have been updated there is no downside.

THE DAMAGE: A simple pricing structure: adults £5, children £2, vehicles £1 and dogs £1 per night. Tents and motorhomes only.

THE FACILITIES: Recently installed are separate toilet blocks and hot water for showers and washing up, and filtered drinking water. A post office and general stores (01229 716255) with its own small gallery can be found 3 miles away in Ulpha, selling newspapers, groceries and paintings.

NEAREST DECENT PUB: The Newfield Inn (01229 716208), 10 minutes' walk down the road in Seathwaite, has real ale, a real fire and hearty food. It's open all day, so if the weather turns treacherous, you can hole up here and try each of the beers one by one. A healthy walk or drive away at Broughton Mills is the Blacksmith's Arms (01229 716824), a classic Lakeland walker's pub, little changed for hundreds of years.

FOOD AND DRINK: Broughton in Furness has a butchers and greengrocers, both of which stock local and organic foods.

IF IT RAINS: Muncaster Castle (01229 717614) near Ravenglass, is allegedly one of Britain's most haunted castles. You can explore the castle grounds, see owls, buzzards and kites, or – if you dare – stay for an overnight 'Ghost Sit' in the haunted Tapestry Room.

TREAT YOURSELF: To some car-free time and walk, walk, walk; just make sure you come with all your supplies.

GETTING THERE: From Great Langdale continue over the high-gradient Wrynose Pass, following signs for Seathwaite. Turner Hall Farm is signposted on the left. The alternative route is via Broughton Mills from the A593. Continue through Seathwaite, and you'll see the campsite signposted on your right.

OPEN: Apr–Oct.

IF IT'S FULL: For a more mainstream, on-the-beaten-track experience in the same area, try Fisherground Campsite (01946 723 349) near Beckfoot, to the west.

Turner Hall Farm, Seathwaite, Broughton in Furness, Cumbria LA20 6EE

| | t | 01229 716420 | w | www.duddonvalley.co.uk |

wasdale head

England's highest mountains may not be on the scale of the Alps, the Andes or the Himalayas, but they are impressive in their own understated way. They also have the advantage of being readily accessible and in most seasons they can be conquered relatively easily with the help of a pair of decent walking boots, favourable weather and a thermos of hot tea.

Several of the country's highest mountains are clustered around the northern end of Wast Water in The Lakes, where the National Trust has thoughtfully sited a camping ground at Wasdale Head. From here, you can lie in a sleeping bag, head poking out of your tent and as the dawn mist clears, you're able to survey the surrounding slopes and plan your ascent on these high fells. Alternatively, you may want to reach for the camping stove and kettle, stay snug in your sleeping bag and enjoy this most vertical of views from your horizontal vantage point.

Most visitors come here to get a bit closer and Wasdale Head is a handy base for Scafell Pike, being the start of one of the gentler ascents on the rock-strewn summit.

Back at base camp there's a small shop for walking maps, friendly advice and blister-shaped plasters. Aside from the shop and the tidy, wooden shower block, facilities are not over-extravagant. Three small fields scattered with mature and planted trees provide plenty of flat grass for pitching, and with cars restricted to the designated parking areas, it's a peaceful site. Definitely a high point on England's campsite circuit.

THE UPSIDE: Top wilderness location for hiking and climbing; great views of the high fells.

THE DOWNSIDE: No prior booking – first come, first served.

THE DAMAGE: Adult £4.50–5.50, child £2–2.50 and a family rate of £11–13.50 per night. Vehicles are £2.50–3. Dogs £1.50.

THE FACILITIES: Hot showers, flush toilets, disabled facilities, laundry and dog-walking area. There's a small shop selling basic food and camping accessories.

NEAREST DECENT PUB: The Wasdale Head Inn (01946 726229), ½ a mile to the north, is reputedly home to the biggest liar in the world (take that with a pinch of salt). And serves hearty, wholesome food for under a tenner.

FOOD AND DRINK: Buy direct from the farmer at Wasdale Head Hall Farm (01946 726245). They rear a large number of Herdwicks (local sheep suited to the harsh conditions on the high fells), as well as a herd of tough, hardy Galloway cattle.

IF IT RAINS: Visit the Roman port of Ravenglass, the only coastal town within the Lake District National Park, or nearby Muncaster Castle (p216).

TREAT YOURSELF: To some tea room goodies or just a bag of flour at Muncaster Watermill (01229 717232), a traditional village mill that's been in operation since 1455.

GETTING THERE: Approaching from the south on the main A595, turn right at Holmrook for Santon Bridge and follow the signs up to Wasdale Head. Approaching from the north, turn left at Gosforth.

OPEN: All year.

IF IT'S FULL: Basic camping facilities are available in a field adjacent to the Wasdale Head Inn, or for a more comfortable stay, head to Church Stile Farm (01946 726252) at the other end of Wast Water.

Wasdale Head National Trust Campsite, Wasdale Head, Seascale, Cumbria CA20 1EX

| t | 01946 726220 | w | www.nationaltrust.org.uk |

syke farm

Technology hasn't arrived at Syke Farm campsite yet, and it's all the better for it. 'We're not into those computers,' says the friendly proprietor Mrs Kyle as she marches officiously around collecting tent fees. 'We didn't put ourselves on the Internet – someone else has put us there'.

It's true. Internet users have been writing glowing reviews about Mrs Kyle's unassuming campsite. And it appears to have caught her off-guard. Whatever next? An entry in *Cool Camping*?

Syke Farm belongs to another age. It's tucked away in a quiet Lake District valley to the southwest of Keswick in the tiny hamlet of Buttermere. It's not just technology that's having trouble making inroads here. Running water is reluctantly offered as an option, with one shower each for men and women. There's no reception or shop – fees are collected promptly at 8am and the only source of provisions is the farmhouse in the village offering eggs and milk. As for entertainment, well there's a dangerous-looking rope-swing.

That's pretty much it – an unpretentious, no-frills campsite with an unapologetically back-to-basics approach. And that's exactly why this place makes you feel like you've travelled back in time, escaping all the luxury and materialism of modern life.

Spend a few days relaxing in Buttermere, gazing into the bubbling beck, eating too many locally made ice creams, and you'll begin to understand Mrs Kyle's perspective. After all, if you find yourself in this glorious spot away from the world, why would you want to be put anywhere else?

THE UPSIDE: Idyllic countryside setting amongst lakes and mountains.

THE DOWNSIDE: Cars not allowed on site; you have to lug your gear across the access bridge.

THE DAMAGE: Price per adult with car is £6 in high season, without car is £5; children £3.

THE FACILITIES: Not much: a couple of showers (50p for 6 minutes) and toilets in a cold stone hut. And there's a shelter with picnic tables.

NEAREST DECENT PUB: Take your pick between The Bridge Hotel (01768 770252) and The Fish Hotel (01768 770253), both of which are just a few minutes' stroll from the campsite and serve real ales and good food. The Bridge Hotel has a pleasant beer garden by the stream.

FOOD AND DRINK: Buttermere Ayrshires Ice Cream at the farm is second to none.

IF IT RAINS: It always rains in the Lake District – bring waterproofs!

TREAT YOURSELF: To another helping of ice cream, see FOOD AND DRINK.

GETTING THERE: Take the B5289 from Keswick for the stunning drive over Honister Pass to Buttermere village. On approaching the village, turn left after the church to get to the car park and Syke Farm.

PUBLIC TRANSPORT: In the summer you can catch the bus from Keswick to Buttermere.

OPEN: All year. Come off-season for extra tranquillity

IF IT'S FULL: The *Cool Camping* site at Wasdale Head (p218) is just south of here. But there are some pretty big mountains in the way, so it's a long drive or a strenuous walk.

Syke Farm Camping Ground, Buttermere, Cumbria CA13 9XA   t   01768 770222

stonethwaite

Civilisation ebbs away, along with your mobile phone signal, as you navigate the long-forgotten, pot-holed, gravel road to Stonethwaite campsite. But the suspension-busting workout rewards your pupils with a narrow hidden valley, lined by scree crags and woodland clinging to the perpendicular sides.

In what's left of the flat ground sits your new home, on a simple patch of grass hugging the river bank. And out here the rumble of the river is the only sound to trouble your mind. Your feet as well as your eyes can wander all over the surrounding contours, with five Wainwrights (a group of 214 hills, made famous by the *Pictorial Guide to the Lakeland Fells* written by Alfred Wainwright) within a mile of the site.

Some may find this site too puritanical in its escape-from-it-all philosophy. There are no showers, and the water from the solitary tap currently has to be boiled (the site's noticeboard will carry the latest advice on the drinkability of the water). But it's a small price to pay for this truly staggering setting.

If cabin fever sets in, then civilisation's comforts are only 6 miles away in Keswick. A menagerie of tea houses, galleries, shops, a cinema and lakeside theatre mean there's something for everyone. Or if you've worn out your feet romping about then go exploring Derwent's shoreline sitting down in your very own rowing boat.

Stonethwaite is a back-to-basics, stripped-down refuge from civilisation. With no showers, drinkable water or mobile phone signal, it may be a step too far for some. But it'll be perfect for others.

THE UPSIDE: Back-to-basics escapism deep in the Cumbrian hills.

THE DOWNSIDE: Possibly too basic for first timers.

THE DAMAGE: £4 per person per night.

THE FACILITIES: Keeping with the back-to-basics theme, there's a small toilet block and a sole tap; the water currently requires pre-boiling before it's safe to drink.

NEAREST DECENT PUB: The homely Langstrath Inn (01768 777239) in Stonethwaite village occupies an old cottage with an exposed beam roof and open fire. All the food and ale is locally sourced – the lamb comes from Yewtree Farm in Rosthwaite, the steak pie uses Limousin beef from the nearby Newlands Valley and they offer a tasty selection of Cumbrian cheeses.

FOOD AND DRINK: Nosh on fine gastro-wares such as Cumbrian air-dried ham or baked Cumbrian cheddar cheese at The Punch Bowl Inn (01539 568237) at Crosthwaite.

IF IT RAINS: Catch a show at the Theatre by the Lake (01768 774411) or pay homage to vehicles used in films and television at Cars of the Stars (01768 773757) both in Keswick.

TREAT YOURSELF: To some good city-living at Morrels (01768 772666). This slick boutique restaurant serves up contemporary cuisine and has luxury apartments for rent to boot.

GETTING THERE: Take the A591 to Keswick, then follow signs for the B5289. Drive approx 7 miles on the B5289, and turn left into Stonethwaite village. Head into the village following the NT signs and follow the gravel road which leads you to the site.

PUBLIC TRANSPORT: Take the 79 bus from Keswick to Stonethwaite. Walk into the village, then directions as above.

OPEN: All year.

IF IT'S FULL: Syke Farm (p220) just over Honiston Pass, in Buttermere, has back-to-basics camping.

Stonethwaite National Trust Campsite, Borrowdale, Keswick, Cumbria CA12 5XG | t | 01768 777234

gillside farm

The phrase 'it's all about location location location' rings true at Gillside Farm. One of the finest views in the Lakes is to be enjoyed standing in the shadow of Helvellyn and looking out across the reaches of Ullswater's valley. Being able to relish such scenes from your tent just adds to the experience.

You'll find Gillside Farm a quarter of a mile up the valley where the track ends, looking over this commanding spectacle. With your dues paid at the farmhouse, you're free to set up camp wherever you like on the field that rolls back down towards Glenridding. Pitch at the bottom of the hill and you'll stare skywards to the surrounding peaks. Pitch at the top and you'll get near-panoramic views into the Ullswater valley. So, it's pretty much win-win for everyone.

Wherever you pitch up though, you'll get close to the residents of this 40-year old working farm. Rabbits and sheep roam unfazed by the temporary squatters and the sound of sheep mowing the lawn around your tent is often your morning wake-up call. Just be careful where you put the food stash.

The stunning setting is enhanced by the small moss-lined beck that runs past the farmhouse and joins the river moving slowly past the site. You can camp within earshot of the bubbling beck, where most campers' kids can be seen splashing around and getting progressively wetter as the day goes by.

For the aspiring Wainwright in you, Gillside Farm is ideally placed to pick off some must-do treks. Running alongside the farm is the track that will take you up to that apex of the Eastern fells, Helvellyn and Striding Edge. The pathway can feel like a major A-road come the weekend, but you can remedy that by pitching further up the hill nearer to the farmhouse and the cover of the lichen walls. But if the call of fells falls on deaf ears then the pathway can also carry you back into town, lower altitudes and less-strenuous activities around the lake's edge. Each day the farm posts an updated five-day weather report in its window, which comes in handy whether you're heading fellwards or lakeside.

Although it's called a caravan and camping park there's no fear of a caravan in sight to spoil that view. The site's split into two, with canvas campers in one field overlooking the valley and the caravans across the road under cover of trees.

If you fancy some farm produce for your stove each morning, then simply head to the farmhouse to restock your larder with fresh milk and eggs. Or, if you're feeling lazy, follow the delicious smell of sizzling sausages and smokey bacon, to find the small hut down by the walking track serving up a hearty English breakfast each morning.

There's easy access from the campsite to Ullswater lake. Time it right, and you can get the boat out to Howtown or Pooley Bridge and walk back to Glenridding around the path along the shoreline. Glenridding itself is a former mining village, which sprung up around the local mines working their way deep within the hillsides. In fact, the nearby Travellers Rest was purpose-built to quench miners' thirst after a day in the dark. If you fancy going underground yourself than you can take a tour down one of the old mines at the Threlkeld Quarry and Mining Museum.

With its picturesque views and easy access to water and walking, Gillside Farm is, in camping terms, a gem as precious as the local stone once was – although thankfully not as costly.

THE UPSIDE: Low-key camping, with outstanding views.

THE DOWNSIDE: The pathway by the site's edge can be an intrusion.

THE DAMAGE: Prices per night are: the pitch £1, adults £6, children (5–16) £3 and vehicle £1.

THE FACILITIES: Hot showers cost 20p, just get in before 9am when the water goes off. There's a toilet block and washroom. Basic provisions are available from the farmhouse shop.

NEAREST DECENT PUB: The Travellers Rest (01768 482298), with views out to Ullswater, is a nice place to end the day. It serves a selection of cask ales, and the 'Travellers Mixed Grill' will satisfy any post-hike appetite.

FOOD AND DRINK: Every third Tuesday Penrith hosts a farmer's market with local mouth-watering specialities.

IF IT RAINS: Uncover the Lakes' mining heritage at Threlkeld Quarry and Mining Museum (01768 779747) near Keswick. You can explore the mines underground or visit the museum above ground.

TREAT YOURSELF: To a night at the movies. The Rheged Centre (01768 868000) in Penrith has a state-of-the-art cinema with 7 IMAX-style movies showing every day on a gigantic screen.

GETTING THERE: Take the A591 to Windermere. Then follow the A592 over Kirkstone Pass to Glenridding. Turn left onto Greenside road and follow the brown signs.

PUBLIC TRANSPORT: From Penrith take the 108 bus to Glenridding town centre. The site is up Greenside Road and is well signposted.

OPEN: Mar–Oct.

IF IT'S FULL: Solitude and good walks can be found at another Cool Camping site – The Quiet Site (p232) – just above Ullswater.

Gillside Farm, Glenridding, Penrith, Cumbria CA11 0QQ

| | t | 01768 482346 | w | www.gillsidecaravanandcampingsite.co.uk |

side farm

Side Farm, on the eastern side of the Lake District, might just be one of the most scenically situated campsites on the planet, sandwiched as it is between the steep slopes of Place Fell to the rear and the sylvan shores of Ullswater at its front. The view across the lake to the Helvellyn Fells is one of the most compelling and beautiful sights in England, and to be able to simply open the tent every morning onto this stunning scene is reason enough to stay a while at Side Farm.

For many, just to sit by the tent with a good book, soaking up the magnificence of the situation, may be sufficient – possibly wandering down to the foot of the site and the shores of Ullswater for a change of perspective. Others arrive with canoes, spending their time paddling the length and breadth of Ullswater, the second largest but most enchanting of the region's lakes. The lake has a rigidly enforced 10 mph speed limit, making this a very safe and well-suited environment for the less hectic forms of waterborne craft.

But if the boating opportunities are superb, and they are, the amazing variety of places to explore on foot from Side Farm is nothing short of astounding. The site lies immediately next to the lakeside path from Howtown to Patterdale, described by Wainwright, the legendary fell walker and guidebook writer, as 'the most beautiful and rewarding in Lakeland'. This is probably the first place to direct your energies, and the most interesting way of completing the walk is said to be by boarding one of the old Ullswater steamers at Glenridding, sailing to Howtown, then strolling back to the site. Undoubtedly a great day out, the sailing out and walking back makes quite an appealing kind of expedition. Unfortunately, at weekends or in high summer, most of humanity seems to find this idea enticing. We may be exaggerating a little bit, but if you like wild and beautiful places to yourself then choose your time or season carefully.

The lakeside path back from Howtown does encounter a few minor ups and downs, but if something more adventurous is on your prescription then walking over Place Fell to Sandwick and using the lakeside path back makes for a more rounded day. The stroll along Boredale to meet up with the Howton–Patterdale path (after an initial fairly steep climb to Boredale Hause) is another great walk from Side Farm.

In the end, however, after staring at the rocky giants across the lake for a few days, the mind will inevitably start to wander up the slopes of Helvellyn – quickly followed by the feet. There are several excellent routes up this most famous of fells from the campsite (enough to keep you busy for a full week on this monster alone) but the one that everybody should do at least once is the dance across the top of Striding Edge. Yes it's popular, and yes it can get scary when the wind is howling around the rocky crest and yes the weather can change from summer to winter in an instant, but this walk is one of the most attention-grabbing and exhilarating in England.

The site itself has flat pitching and adequate facilities including toilets and showers, but luxurious they are not and can be somewhat overwhelmed when the site is full. But bring a pair of walking boots, or a canoe, and the idyllic location will more than compensate for any minor niggles.

THE UPSIDE: Perhaps the most scenically placed campsite in England with an unbeatable selection of walks.
THE DOWNSIDE: Too many people know about the upside.
THE DAMAGE: Adults £5, children £3, cars £2. Tents and small motorhomes only.
THE FACILITIES: Reasonable amenities with toilets, showers and laundry. And a tea room.
NEAREST DECENT PUB: The White Lion Inn (01768 482214) at Patterdale, 15 minutes' walk from the campsite, has a traditional appeal, dependable bar food and tasty home-made soup.

FOOD AND DRINK: If you're looking for something tasty to slap on the barbie, then look no further than the mini-market in Glenridden, which sells local meats.
IF IT RAINS: A variety of lake cruises are offered by Ullswater Steamers (01768 482229), or a cinema and a national Mountaineering Exhibition can be found at Rheged (01768 868000).
TREAT YOURSELF: To some time off two feet at Rookin House Equestrian and Activity Centre (01768 483561). Choose from horse riding and quad biking to fishing and human bowling(!).

GETTING THERE: From Junction 40 of the M6 take the A66 west, then the A592 along the shore of Ullswater through Glenridding. One mile beyond Glenridding centre, turn left into a track to Side Farm – just after the church on the right.
PUBLIC TRANSPORT: From Penrith you can catch a bus to Patterdale and then it's a short walk.
OPEN: Easter–Oct.
IF IT'S FULL: Good sites nearby include Sykeside Camping Park (01768 482239) at Brotherswater and Gillside Farm (p224) at Glenridding.

| **Side Farm Campsite**, Patterdale, Penrith, Cumbria CA11 0NP | t | 01768 482337 |

the quiet site

It's an unusual name for a campsite, the Quiet Site – an over-promise that can surely only disappoint. We were expecting to have to communicate in silent sign language and walk around in slippers, and if the wind picked up to hold the sides of the tent and save them flapping noisily in the breeze. The reality is that this place isn't much quieter than your average campsite. But the name is enough to put off any rowdies or big groups, so it's certainly quieter than some of the more boisterous Lake District options.

Standing atop the fells of what many hold as the Lakes' finest water, the Quiet Site looks down to Ullswater's mist-shrouded surface. Up here, it's a peaceful escape from the hustle and bustle of Glenridding town; a sanctuary of calm from the Lakeland summer crowds.

The site is ideal for accessing the peace of the Lakes' pathways, with several walkways passing close by. On arrival you'll get a handcrafted walking guide with decent walks around the area popped into your hand. The walks link up with spectacular lake views, natural wonders, such as the gushing waterfalls at Aria Force, and local historic spots, such as Lowther Castle, plus the local watering holes.

They've tailored the walks to all family members and interests. So, you should find one that suits you – whether it's a full-on lung workout up the fells or an amble with the kids. And if you've had your fill of biped pursuits, go amphibious to get a watery perspective of Ullswater either from the famous Ullswater Steamer or from a rowing boat or motorboat, both easily hired at Watermillock or Glenridding marina.

Come the end of the day, you don't even have to make any effort to lay your hands on a well-earned pint. The Quiet Site has its own public house, simply named 'The Pub'. Housed in the farm's original stone barn, a roaring open hearth greets you along with the über-friendly hosts and a raft of local ales. Inside the décor is certainly unique. Part curio-shop, part-taxidermy exhibit, part-Hammer horror film set, it exudes a one-of-a-kind charm that you'd be hard pressed to unearth in any other pub in Britain, let alone a campsite. Unfortunately, if you're looking to escape campsite cooking you'll be disappointed: they don't do food.

Whilst the Quiet Site aims to please everyone, there's a huge family focus with a massive adventure playground and playrooms in 'The Pub' that could even bring out the kid in the grown-up within your group. And, with a pet-walking field as well, there's no worries if you've brought your four-legged friend either.

All the tent sites are terraced into the hill, so despite the incline you'll be as straight as a spirit level come bedtime. The pitches' design also offers good wind protection.

Up here you escape the ambient light pollution at night from the surrounding towns. You'll gaze skywards in awe at the dazzling Milky-Way-strewn skies – clouds permitting. But being so far from civilisation can have its drawbacks, too; you can get cabin fever. And it's about a 30-minute drive back to Glenridding, so

walking for provisions or a change of night-time venue is pretty much off the agenda.

Nearby Pooley Bridge offers a reprieve if the elements turn on you, and its armoury of scone-toting tea rooms will help you pile on the pounds (supplies for future walks, you can tell yourself) whilst you while away the day. You can reach the town by car or by the more scenic route on the Ullswater Steamer.

If you're looking for some serenity, great walking or just want to kick back with the family, the Quiet Site delivers. With this place having a hardcore following, and attracting more by the year, just try to keep it all a little hush-hush.

THE UPSIDE: Starry nights and quiet days away from it all.

THE DOWNSIDE: Having to pack all you need to avoid long supply drives.

THE FACILITIES: There's an on-site pub, free hot showers, washing-up area and small shop with all the basics.

THE DAMAGE: Flat pitches from £17–27 per night; standard pitches (slightly sloped) £12–22. Prices include 1 tent, 1 car and 2 adults. Children (5–15) are £2 per night, 16s and over £3 and under-4s go free. Dogs are £1 a night.

NEAREST DECENT PUB: The on-site pub serves a variety of local ales but no food. But if you're

after some dinner then head to the Brackenrigg Inn (01768 486206) overlooking Ullswater for above-average grub with a change of scenery.

FOOD AND DRINK: On the shores of Lake Ullswater, the Sharrow Bay Hotel (01768 486301) has a Michelin-starred restaurant. You can do lunch or dinner but they're famous for afternoon teas.

IF IT RAINS: Catch the Ullswater Steamer from Glenridding to Pooley Bridge (01768 482229) or indeed just enjoy the cruise around the lake. History bods may want to explore nearby Dalemain House (01768 486450).

TREAT YOURSELF: To a pampering amongst 67 acres of Windermere's woodland at The Samling

(01539 431922), which persuaded Wordsworth to part with his crowns. Two-night stays cost from £200 to £520, depending on the room.

GETTING THERE: On the A66 to Keswick, take the A592 toward Glenridding, turning right at the Brackenrigg Inn. The site is 1¼ mile on your right.

PUBLIC TRANSPORT: At Penrith board a 106 bus toward Glenridding. Get off outside the Brackenrigg Inn and follow the lane that runs beside the inn, the site is 1¼ mile further along on your right.

OPEN: Mar–mid-Jan.

IF IT'S FULL: Make a beeline to Gillside Farm (p224) in Glenridding for a retreat below Helvellyn.

The Quiet Site, Ullswater, Cumbria CA11 0LS | t | 07768 727016 | w | www.thequietsite.co.uk

hadrian's wall

In AD122, Northumberland represented the farthest reaches of the Roman Empire under Emperor Hadrian. These were turbulent times: everyone wanted to take a pop at Rome's dominance and to try to grab a slice of land when the administrators weren't looking. The Picts, the wild tribes of Caledonia in today's Scotland, were particularly troublesome. So, Hadrian decided to protect his empire by building a wall around it. His stone construction is 73 miles long and five metres high, and stretches from the Tyne to the Solway Firth.

The years have weathered Hadrian's Wall, now a UNESCO World Heritage Site, but the ruins of this historic structure remain impressive and atmospheric. It's easy to imagine how the soldiers here must have felt, keeping watch at the very outpost of the civilised world.

The military barracks along the wall are long gone, but you can still camp just a mile or so from one of the most dramatic sections of the wall at Hadrian's Wall Campsite. The site is terraced on four levels and there's an overflow meadow on a lower slope, where there's more space to spread out, although the facilities are back at the main site.

The campsite is well-located for walks along Hadrian's Wall Path, an 84-mile National Trail that shadows the line of the wall. Campsite owners Graham and Patricia will even arrange transport to or from your starting or finishing points, leaving you to enjoy your walk and the wall.

THE UPSIDE: A beautiful countryside campsite near Hadrian's Wall.

THE DOWNSIDE: It's a small site, so pitches can be a bit close together. Only two showers each for males and females.

THE DAMAGE: Backpacker £6, tent and car £8 plus £2 per person and caravan/trailer tent £10.

THE FACILITIES: There's a new shower/toilet block with hairdryers, disabled facilities, a sauna, a campers' fridge/freezer; the washing machine, tumble dryer, eggs and tinned groceries are subject to an 'honesty box' system. Order the night before for a full English breakfast; BBQ meat packs also available.

NEAREST DECENT PUB: The stone-built Milecastle Inn (01434 321372), a mile to the west, has everything an age-old country pub could want including wooden beams covered in nick-nacks, an open fire and a resident ghost. It also has the benefit of 'wall' views from the beer garden.

FOOD AND DRINK: The Raysons at Herding Hill Farm (01434 320668) breed rare Dexter cattle, Berkshire pigs and Shropshire lambs on their small hill farm, just off the Military Road. And in late 2006, they opened their farm shop/café and bistro to sell their own produce.

IF IT RAINS: The Housesteads Roman Fort and Museum (01434 344363), the best-preserved Roman fort in Britain, is just down the road.

GETTING THERE: The campsite is located just east of Haltwhistle. From the B6318 Military Road, take the turning to Melkridge. The site is just 300 metres on the left. From the A69, 1 mile east of Haltwhistle, there's a staggered crossroads at Melkridge village. Take the turning opposite the village and continue for 2 miles.

PUBLIC TRANSPORT: The campsite owners can collect you from Haltwhistle train station or from nearby bus stops, check when you book.

OPEN: All year.

IF IT'S FULL: About 15 miles to the north is Kielder Camping site (01434 250291) – a remote and peaceful location from which to explore.

Hadrian's Wall Campsite, Melkridge Tilery, nr Haltwhistle, Northumberland NE49 9PG

| t | 01434 320495 | w | www.romanwallcamping.co.uk |

demesne farm

It all started with an irate local bobby one night in 1972. Presented with yet another duo of wayward Pennine Way walkers knocking on his door in the late hours asking for accommodation advice, the camel's back broke. The then local constable appealed to Tom at Demesne Farm in the twilight hours to take them off his hands and put them up for the night.

The farm's bottom field became their overnight home. Next, came a sign, then more tents and it all grew from there. Thirty-six years later, Tom, the family and the farm are still here, playing host to to a regular influx of walkers and campers.

Demesne Farm's patch of flat green sits on the outskirts of the sleepy blink-and-you'll-miss-it-village of Bellingham. The campsite itself is not that large, with only one field given over to campers, but it feels bigger than it is as it looks out over a wide expanse of rural England that glows golden as the sun falls. The farm is very popular with groups and can get quite busy in the summer months, but there's an overflow field to ease any congestion and keep disruption to a minimum.

The facilities reside in a partially converted barn inside the barnyard, past hay bales and a large chicken coop. Farms may not be the

tidiest places, but these facilities are mucked out as sure as the cock crows every morning. But this is about as close to the farm's day-to-day workings as you'll come, the rest is shielded by the dry-stone walls and kept strictly for the professionals. The smells, though, manage to make their way into the site, so there's still a farmyard atmosphere and you're almost guaranteed to come into close contact with some of the farm's resident animals. Completely undeterred by the presence of campers, there's an inquisitive brood of chickens that like to scrabble around your guide ropes taking a peck out of anything in reach. They are a firm favourite of all who visit here.

From the campsite you can head out along the near-endless Pennine Way, which passes by the site's gate. Or if you're in the saddle, then Bellingham sits on the Reivers Way cycle route as it cuts its way from Tynemouth in the East to Whitehaven on the West Coast.

Bellingham itself has little to offer. Kielder Water is the main draw here, a mere eight miles away across the moors. As Northern Europe's largest artificial lake, its 27 miles of shoreline boasts a multitude of activities: (first take a deep breath) there's windsurfing, sailing, canoeing, fishing, cycling and walking, lake cruises, miles of self-guided walks and ever-expanding mountain-bike trails throughout the forest. And, now, breathe again.

Walking around Kielder Forest's moss-carpeted innards you stand a good chance of coming across the minute, tufted ears of the embattled native red squirrel. The dense forests here are the species' last real stronghold in the UK, with 75% of the UK's populace residing here.

It used to be said that all roads lead to Rome. But around here, it's more like all roads lead to a Roman ruin. The World Heritage listed Hadrian's heathen-blocking wall snakes across the landscape around Bellingham and nearby Hexham. Many sections of the wall are only a short drive away and several sites are easily reachable in a day trip.

These days, policing the locals doesn't involve walls and forts, just a few friendly bobbies on the beat. It may not be a hotbed of crime, but one fine officer surely deserves a medal, for services to camping.

THE UPSIDE: Quiet farm retreat.

THE DOWNSIDE: It occasionally gets busy with groups, which can affect the ambience.

THE DAMAGE: A car, tent and 2 people cost £10 per night. Car, tent and 1 person is £6 per night. Under 5s are free, children (6–15) are £2 and extra adults £4.50.

THE FACILITIES: There are separate toilet and shower blocks; showers cost 50p. Plus, there's washing-up facilities. That's it.

NEAREST DECENT PUB: Don't hold your breath. The Cheviot Hotel (01434 220696) offers moderate Northumberland sustenance, but it's nothing to get excited about. On Main Street in Bellingham, you'll find the working men's clubs of Black Bull (01434 220226) and the Rose & Crown (01434 673263).

FOOD AND DRINK: Kielder Organic Meats (01434 220 435), on Bellingham's outskirts sells organic produce, both meaty and vegetable-y. Or head to Hexham Market (see IF IT RAINS).

IF IT RAINS: Visit Hexham, a nearby historic market town, whose 1300-year-old Abbey still hosts the town's market in its shadow every Tuesday and Saturday.

TREAT YOURSELF: To a slap-up meal at the acclaimed Riverdale Hall Hotel (01434 220254) on the outskirts of Bellingham, where you can savour pan-seared tuna or chicken breast stuffed with mozzarella.

GETTING THERE: Leave the A69 at Acomb and take the A6079 to Chollerford then join the B6320 towards Bellingham. In Bellingham turn right at Lloyds TSB Bank, the campsite is 100 metres on the right.

PUBLIC TRANSPORT: From Hexham take the 880 bus, which stops in Bellingham. Follow the road that runs beside Lloyds TSB bank for 100 metres, the farm's on the right.

OPEN: May–Oct/Nov.

IF IT'S FULL: Head to Hadrian's Wall campsite near Haltwhistle (p236) for a beautiful countryside setting and yep you guessed it – the wall.

Demesne Farm, Bellingham, Hexham, Northumberland NE48 2BS				
	t	01434 220258	w	www.demesnefarmcampsite.co.uk

beadnell bay

There is something strange and ever-so-slightly out of kilter about the north Northumberland coast, which is much easier to sense in the air, or feel under your feet, than put your finger on by mere expression. It's almost as if time is travelling on a different plane – that something of the past is constantly reaching forwards through invisible chasms in the layers of time. Or perhaps the present is reaching back. It may just be that this remote coastal strip remains as it has been for hundreds of years, and that the only real signs of development are a collection of amazing fortresses built nearly a thousand years ago.

Just in case you aren't sure whereabouts in England this unchanging oasis of tranquillity and beauty lies, it's in the far northeastern corner of the country, very nearly in Scotland. At the moment it's in England, but you never know around here.

Beadnell Bay campsite, situated next to the sea at Beadnell Bay, is about two miles south of Seahouses – surely the smallest seaside resort in the world. Small it may very well be, but Seahouses boasts a couple of pubs, a couple of chippies and a working fishing harbour, with boats running out to

visit the famous Farne Islands – home of birds, but nothing (nor anybody) else. The village of Beadnell itself even has a chip shop and a pub to sustain the active camping life, so what more can you ask for?

The site would be best described as unremarkable in itself, with a flat featureless field presenting nothing in the way of shelter to soften the occasionally wicked east wind from pummelling your tent. Facilities too are fairly average, but there is everything you need in the ablutional department to keep visitors from becoming social outcasts. However, all this is unimportant really, for nobody comes here to sit and ponder how glamorous the toilet block is, or isn't. To come here is to fall under the spell of the empty coastline, and the history still trembling through the air.

What you will definitely need at Beadnell Bay is your bike, for these quiet, level back roads all along the coast are perfect for velocopedic exploration. The first place to explore is the coast road through Seahouses to Bamburgh. Pedalling out of Seahouses will give you a first ethereal glimpse of Bamburgh Castle – miles away, piercing the heavens, and apparently floating on sand. As the miles disappear under your wheels this hazy mirage gradually solidifies into an elegant but enormous red edifice, impressive and noble in the soft Northumberland sun.

Further north is the Holy Island of Lindisfarne, cut off at high tide, and where, if there really is a time leak occurring hereabouts, the epicentre will surely be found in the ruined priory, or looking out from the harbour scanning the coast from Lindisfarne Castle southwards, to where Bamburgh mysteriously stands.

Despite all this beauty and excitement, the real thrill of this coast is to walk south from the campsite along the sands, past Beadnell Bay, Newton Haven and the empty, exotic-looking Embleton Bay, to take in the dramatic views of Dunstanburgh Castle. Although you probably will be drawn towards the atmospheric ruins, there's no need to get any closer to confirm that something is indeed going on in the ether, and to feel a deep and magnetic attraction to this deserted landscape and seascape.

THE UPSIDE: A stunning stretch of deserted coastline.

THE DOWNSIDE: No direct views from the site; a minor road runs next to the campsite.

THE DAMAGE: Adults £4.40–6.95 per night, children £2.15–2.25, non-members additional £6 per night pitch fee; tents and motorhomes only.

THE FACILITIES: Decent facilities with toilets, disabled toilet and shower, unmetered showers and washing-up sinks; gas refills at reception.

NEAREST DECENT PUB: If you're desperate, The Craster Arms (01665 720272) is a mere

5 minutes' walk away in Beadnell, but a more worthwhile journey is to The Ship Inn (01665 576262) at Low Newton-by-the-Sea, a lovely, well-managed pub with a menu rich in local seafood.

FOOD AND DRINK: Head to Swallow Fish Ltd (01665 721052) in Seahouses for supplies of local wet fish, including crab and sea bass.

IF IT RAINS: If you've done all the castles including Bamburgh (01668 214515), Alnwick (01665 510777) and Dunstanburgh (01665 576231), then see what's on at the Alnwick Playhouse (01665 510785).

TREAT YOURSELF: To a breakfast fit for a king – Craster kippers from L. Robson & Sons Ltd (01665 576223).

GETTING THERE: From the A1, 5 miles north of Alnwick, take the B6347 east then the B1340 to Beadnell. The site is on the left after a bend to the north of Beadnell.

OPEN: Apr–Oct.

IF IT'S FULL: The Camping and Caravanning Club also have a good site 6 miles south at Dunstan Hill (01665 576310).

Beadnell Bay Campsite, Beadnell, Chathill, Northumberland NE67 5BX

	t	01665 720586	w	www.campingandcaravanningclub.co.uk

pot-a-doodle do

Sounding like some weird kind of experiment with a cockerel and a ready meal, Pot-a-doodle do also looks a bit whacky. Imagine if you will, a small collection of tipis and wooden wigams sitting on the Northumberland coast; it looks like a geographically misplaced scene from a Western. Now, if you're up for some cowboys and Indians, let's get rolling, rolling, rolling...

Each of the eight wigwams sleeps up to five people and is powered by an electric hook-up, providing heat, light and a small fridge. And when the North Sea decides to teach the land who's boss, you'll be thankful you're under something sturdier than canvas.

The four tipis are more basic: decked out inside with futons and candles, but slightly lacking on traditional designs. That said, the kids will love them. The site is family focused, with supervised activities galore in its creative art centre and cross-country Quad biking for a range of ages.

Nearby tidal Holy Island holds many attractions, but make sure you check the tide times in advance to save yourself and your car from a dip in the sea. Lindisfarne Castle, built by the monastic demolition expert Henry VIII, who pillaged stone from the now skeletal local priory, sits atop a volcanic mound at the island's end and looks imperiously out to sea.

You, too, can venture seaward for some ornithologist action on the Farne Islands – one of the UK's top seabird sanctuaries, colonised by thousands of puffins, dive-bomber terns and guillemots. It's probably a good idea to wear a hat for protection. (Preferably not of the cowboy variety).

THE UPSIDE: Cowboy-and-Indian family camping.
THE DOWNSIDE: Couples may prefer the tipis but there's only four of them.
THE DAMAGE: Wigwams: £14.50–18.50 per night, depending on season, and children £8–10. Tipis: £50 per night for up to 4 people, then it's £10 per adult and £5 per child thereafter.
THE FACILITIES: There's a well-equipped kitchen, on-site shop, laundry room, free hot showers, interactive art centre and children's play area.
NEAREST DECENT PUB: The Barrels Ale House (01289 308013), in Berwick-upon-Tweed, hosts a

selection of local cask ales and live music but is a 20-minute drive away.
FOOD AND DRINK: Drink Lindisfarne Mead at St Aidan's Winery (01289 389230). Or there's the farmer's market in Berwick-Upon-Tweed's the Maltings (01289 330999) on the last Sunday of every month.
IF IT RAINS: Head to Holy Island's Lindisfarne Castle, the abbey or tea shops, just mind the tides!
TREAT YOURSELF: To a cruise. The sight and sound of 150,000 birds on the Farne Islands is unforgettable. Boats leave regularly from the seaside town of Seahouses.

GETTING THERE: Leave the A1 at the roundabout signposted Scremerston. After 500 yards turn right towards Scremerston. Take the next left towards Cocklawburn Beach, the site is half a mile on the left.
PUBLIC TRANSPORT: Take a train to Berwick-Upon-Tweed and get a taxi out to the site, no buses currently run near the site.
OPEN: All year.
IF IT'S FULL: Head to the *Cool Camping* site in Beadnell Bay (p242) for a beach location, with stunning coastal views over deserted sands.

Pot-a-Doodle Do, Borewell Farm, Scremerston, Berwick-Upon-Tweed TD15 2RJ

	t	01289 307107	w	www.northumbrianwigwams.com	

festival fun

Summertime and the living is easy. Actually, if we're honest, choosing how to fill our sunbeam days isn't quite as easy as it once was. Back when most of us were young, we'd bundle into the family wagon for a day trip to the beach, explore a castle or stately home or visit a wildlife park – all of this activity peaking with the annual street party or garden fête. Depending on where we lived, obsessing over steel bands through a cloud of candy floss was the norm for hip young Brits. Nowadays, what do kids of all ages consider to be their summer highlight? Festivals. Which is where the difficult part comes in…

Our island is teeming with festivals, aimed at everyone from surfers to samba dancers, cheese-fanatics to laureates. We're spoiled for choice. In turn, the recent surge of new festivals has competitively raised the bar, so now even the range of entertainment is overwhelming. If you don't get a ticket for one of England's major music festivals – such as Glastonbury, Reading or the V Festival, which all sell out within hours – you can still cherry-pick from a glossy catalogue of alternatives.

Kick-starting the season is the Sunrise Celebration. Still very much in its infancy, its popularity is growing fast, helped no end by its proximity to Stonehenge, where thousands of people used to congregate to celebrate the summer solstice. Drawing on Glastonbury's original, free-spirited vibe, organisers concentrate on adhering to a strict environmentally friendly policy. Horse-drawn carts, a solar-powered cinema, classes in spiritual enlightenment and pianos plonked randomly in the fields are amongst their many intriguing attractions.

Mid-July is the height of festival season when you can rave or rock voraciously at events all over the country. We've selected a few that ooze campsite charisma. In a Victorian garden surrounded by Nepalese pagodas and resident peacocks is the 5000-capacity Larmer Tree Festival, opened each year by Jools Holland alongside a full band. Full-ticket holders get to camp for five nights, enjoying wonderful views and five stages of world, folk, roots, blues, jazz, Americana, country and reggae music. It's very eclectic, inoffensive and relaxing. Assorted workshops invite you to try out your singing or carnival costume-making skills, and at night you can dance your socks off in the 'Club Larmer' tent, which stays open until 4am.

Fifty miles further south is the new kid on the festival block – Camp Bestival – which was gearing up for its 2008 launch as we went to press. Lulworth Castle is the stunning setting for its debut, where glimpses of the Jurassic Coast flash in the horizon. Radio 1's Rob da Bank and his Bestival cohorts (Bestival is his September event on the Isle of Wight) aim to offer guests as much fun camping as is humanly possible. Performers dressed as Blue Coats – in tribute to the Red Coats hosts of 1950s holiday camps – will pied piper everyone into a state of joyful camaraderie. Elsewhere, big eclectic and indie rock artists will play numerous stages and daft goings-on will be the order of the day. It'll be very much like Bestival but for all generations to enjoy.

Latitude bounced onto the festival circuit in 2006, nestling into the gorgeous county of Suffolk for its 20,000-capacity, laid-back, artistic venture. With his unrivalled experience in running festivals, the veteran promoter Melvin Benn knows exactly what the audience want: value-for-money live performers plus intellectually challenging (or, at least, thought-provoking) literary stimulation. The biggest names in comedy host the comedy tent where at night the baton is passed to various cabaret and DJ entertainers.

The first weekend in August has traditionally been the UK's hottest weekend on record for many years. The Big Chill has that and the beautiful Eastnor Deer Park site to thank for instilling infectious good moods and bringing out the nicest side in everybody who attends. (Anyone not in a great mood only has to book in for a revitalising Body & Soul treatment.) Culturally, the organisers mix visual art with comedy, story-telling and spoken word. Musically, there's a wide range of traditional to modern artists to discover. When the speakers are switched off, an outdoor cinema, a Media Mix tent and a 24-hour café keep ticking gently through the night. As their website says: for many, The Big Chill is simply the best 100 hours of their year.

Not everyone will have heard of Shambala, yet. The general consensus is that it's one of the most authentically uncommercial festivals in the country. Five friends launched the event for their friends and families in Bristol, moving it in 2007 to Northamptonshire to meet popular demand. Regulars have been outdoing each other in the fancy dress stakes during its entire 10-year history. In fact, audience participation is key to having a good time here, and Shambala's cool community spirit owes much to the non-materialistic nature of the punters they attract. Music isn't the main priority, but everyone seems too content with the enchanting hot tubs, art trails, hammocks and 'aliens on stilts' to care.

festival details

WHAT: **Sunrise Celebration**

WHERE: Yeovil, Somerset

WHEN: Last weekend in May

WHO: People devoted to building sustainable communities, regulars to Glastonbury during the eighties, travellers, new-age hippies, cider guzzlers

WHY: For an authentically grass roots vibe

WWW: www.sunrisecelebration.com

WHAT TO BRING: A 'green' mind – everything at the event is run via renewable energy

CAMPING: There's a long flat field to camp on and, whilst the haystacks might look nice, camp further away from them because they're actually the loos

WHAT: **Larmer Tree Festival**

WHERE: Cranborne Chase, Dorset

WHEN: Mid-July

WHO: Locals, families, regulars (it'll be 20 years old in 2010), Jools Holland fans, real-ale drinkers

WHY: Start your stay with polished rhythm and blues in an idyllic Victorian pleasure garden

WWW: www.larmertreefestival.co.uk

WHAT TO BRING: A big rug, to spread out on the lawns

CAMPING: There's a general field with tipis and disabled camping facilities, a site for day-ticket holders, a camper van area and a shop selling groceries, papers and camping essentials

WHAT: **Camp Bestival**

WHERE: Lulworth Castle, Dorset

WHEN: Mid-July

WHO: Happy campers who love Bestival (see www.bestival.net), fun-loving social butterflies

WHY: Because camping is all the rage, of course!

WWW: www.campbestival.net

WHAT TO BRING: A gramophone, a picnic basket and a random musical instrument to join the 'biggest ever' marching band competition

CAMPING: It might be called Camp Bestival, but taking your own tent isn't a priority, you can also hire tipis, yurts, gypsy caravans, pods, airstreams…

WHAT: Latitude

WHERE: Southwold, Suffolk

WHEN: Mid-July

WHO: Creative types, big name bands, middle-aged bohemians

WHY: Suffolk is a jolly lovely place and it's also on the way to Norfolk, so stop off as part of a longer holiday

WWW: www.latitudefestival.co.uk

WHAT TO BRING: A literary novel to carry around, it'll be a good conversation opener

CAMPING: As at all festivals, don't take any valuables. Keep any you do take on you, and sleep on top of them at night. That way you'll avoid losing out to opportunist thieves

WHAT: The Big Chill

WHERE: Eastnor Castle, Herefordshire

WHEN: First weekend in August

WHO: Londoners, arty types, broad-minded musos, cute toddlers, cocktail queens, head-down groovers

WHY: Immerse yourself in all types of culture at the UK's prettiest festival site

WWW: www.bigchill.net

WHAT TO BRING: Sun cream, they've enjoyed an excellent run of fabulous weather here

CAMPING: The Quiet Camping field has the best views of the valley, whilst late-night revellers should head to the North Camping field. Cafés will feature in all campsites and the family area has a playground

WHAT: Shambala

WHERE: Northamptonshire

WHEN: The last Bank Holiday weekend in August

WHO: Blissed-out friendly faces, older kids who love it as much as the adults

WHY: Say you were at the best kept secret on the festival circuit, before its popularity explodes

WWW: www.shambalafestival.org

WHAT TO BRING: A participating mind and a charismatic demeanour

CAMPING: They have a noise curfew in the campsites, no noise after midnight, plus there's a family information reception

top tips

First timer? Take a minute to read our top tips. Most of it's just common sense, but you never know what you don't know.

WATCH THE WEATHER

The weather can mean the difference between a great trip and an awful trip. Keep an eye on the forecast, and if it's bad, consider postponing. Better to be a proud fair-weather camper than a miserable, moaning wet one.

AVOID SCHOOL HOLIDAYS

Don't go during busy periods if you can help it. Your experience and enjoyment will be greatly enhanced. If you can only go during school holidays, try to opt for quieter sites off the beaten track.

BE PREPARED

More than just a motto! Make sure you've thought through everything you need to take. If it's your first time, make a thorough checklist before you go. A handy checklist can be downloaded at: www.coolcamping.co.uk

CHOOSE A GOOD SITE

Well obviously, it should be a campsite recommended by *Cool Camping*. But within the site, choose exactly where you pitch your tent carefully. Opt for level ground, ideally with some shade, too – tents get very hot in direct sunshine. But make sure your level ground isn't at the bottom of a big dip that will fill with water if it rains. Also, try to pick a place that's near enough to the amenities to be handy, but far enough to be free from associated noise and traffic.

LEAVE NO TRACE

Dispose of your rubbish in the right place, only light fires in designated areas, respect the countryside and don't hassle or feed the wildlife. Lecture over!

happy campers?

We hope you've enjoyed reading *Cool Camping: England* and that it's inspired you to get out there.

The campsites featured in this book are a personal selection chosen by the *Cool Camping* team. None of the campsites has paid a fee for inclusion, nor was one requested, so you can be sure of an objective choice of sites and honest descriptions.

We have visited hundreds of campsites across England to find these, and we hope you like them as much as we do. However, it hasn't been possible to visit every single English campsite. So, if you know of a special place that you think should be included, we'd like to hear about it.

Send us an email telling us the name and location of the campsite, some contact details and why it's special. We'll credit all useful contributions in the next edition and the best emails will receive a complimentary copy. Thanks and see you out there!

england@coolcamping.co.uk

Cool Camping: England (2nd edition)
Series Concept & Series Editor: Jonathan Knight
Researched, written and photographed by: Jonathan Knight, Paul Marsden, Andy Stothert, Xenia Gregoriadis, Sue Newman & Sam Pow
Editor: Nikki Sims
Proofreaders: Jessica Cowie & Shellani Gupta
Design and artwork: Andrew Davis
Production: Catherine Greenwood, Andrew Davis
PR: The Farley Partnership
Coordinator-in-Chief: Catherine Greenwood

Published by: Punk Publishing, 3 The Yard, Pegasus Place, London SE11 5SD

Distributed by:
Portfolio Books, Unit 5, Perivale Industrial Park, Perivale, Middlesex UB6 7RL

All photographs © Jonathan Knight/Paul Marsden/ Andy Stothert/Xenia Gregoriadis/Sue Newman/Sam Pow except the following (all reproduced with permission): Minack Theatre (p25) © Minack Theatre, Porthcurno; view at dusk from Bay View Farm (p45) © Mel Gigg; Lundy Island campsite (p56), Lundy Island (p56) © Lundy Island; Isle of Wight (p100) © Isle of Wight Tourism; Sussex Tipis (pp116–119) © Ken Boyter; Clippesby Hall (pp132–135) © Paul Studd/Clippesby Hall; Deepdale Farm (pp140–143) © Collina Greenwell; additional photos of Feather Down Farm (p147) © Feather Down Farm; Forest of Dean and Cathedral Sculpture (p148) © Isobel Cameron/Forestry Commission; Eastnor Castle (p157) © Martin Avery and James Hervey-Bathurst; Longnor Wood flower meadow (p169), Longnor Wood flower detail (p169) both © Longnor Wood; Beadnell Bay campsite (p242) © The Camping and Caravanning Club; Bestival camper (p248) © Jamie Baker Photography; all other festival shots (p251–p253) reproduced by kind permission of the respective festivals.

Front cover: Henry's campsite, Cornwall © Andy Stothert (lakelandscapes.co.uk)

Many of the photographs featured in this book are available for licensing. For more information, see www.coolcamping.co.uk

The publishers and authors have done their best to ensure the accuracy of all information in *Cool Camping England*, however, they can accept no responsibility for any injury, loss, or inconvenience sustained by anyone as a result of information contained in this book.

Punk Publishing takes its environmental responsibilities seriously. This book has been printed on paper made from renewable sources and we continue to work with out printers to reduce our overall environmental impact. Wherever possible, we recycle, eat organic food and always turn the tap off when brushing our teeth.

A BIG THANK YOU! Thanks to everyone who has written and emailed with feedback, comments and suggestions. It's good to see so many people at one with the *Cool Camping* ethos. In particular, thanks to the following readers for telling us about their favourite places to camp: Catherine Ashton, Sophia Atkinson, Ian Barnett, James Bartlett, Lesley Barton, Mark Beardsley, Jill Beaumont, Tim Bell, Ian Bennett, Simon Bird, Jillian Blackshaw, Helena Blakemore, Rob Boardman, Amanda Boorman, Jennifer Britt, Clara Bulteel, Merryn Butler, Dan Campling, Tracy Cheung, Nancy Claxton, Kerry Coghlan, Tom Crofts, Louise Crowe, Sonja Daniel, Sain Darvill, Jennifer Dovey, Neil Dyble, Cathy Fagan, Claire Field, Caroline Foreman, David Hall, Liz Hennessey, Jood Milne Home, Laura Howell, Kate Husher, Nicky Jones, Marianne Kantor, Duncan King, David Lee, Hannah Leigh, Jo Lewis, Diane Marshall, Gina Martin, Paul Mayer, Andrew McGill, Rachel Mchale, Kerry Mellor, Nick Moore, Jenny Morecombe, Caoimhe O'Neill, Sarah Parkinson, Lisa Peacock, Lisa Pearce, Tim Peplow, George Price, Tom Richardson, Susan Ruttley, Karen Sills, Ben Thackwell, Julie Townsend, Juliana Tramontana, Hannah Webster, Issy Whatmore, Diane Wickens, Laurie Wills, Liz Wood, Paul Woods, Sarah Wright, Alice, Jal, Ben, Jeffrey, Lorraine and Mark, Merryn, Marianne, Sian, Vicky and Liv.